SPEAK OUT ON RAPE!

SPEAK OUT ON RAPE!

MARGARET O. HYDE

McGraw-Hill Book Company

*New York   St. Louis   San Francisco   Auckland
Düsseldorf   Johannesburg   Kuala Lumpur   London
Mexico   Montreal   New Delhi   Panama   Paris
São Paulo   Singapore   Sydney   Tokyo   Toronto*

Book Design by Marcy J. Katz

Library of Congress Cataloging in Publication Data

Hyde, Margaret Oldroyd, date.
  Speak out on rape!

  Bibliography: p.
  Includes index.
  SUMMARY: Provides information for those who want to prevent rape, help its victims, and break the stereotype of the rapist, including discussions on rape crisis centers, hotlines, and outdated laws and ways to change them.
    1. Rape—Juvenile literature. 2. Rape—Prevention—Juvenile literature. [1. Rape] I. Title.
  HV6558.H9   364.1'53   75-10916
  ISBN 0-07-031636-8 lib. bdg.

12345678 MUBP 789876

For the women who had the courage to speak out on rape to me and to the world with the hope that this book may help prevent others from having experiences such as theirs.

Contents

Acknowledgments

Some of the studies mentioned in this book are so new that they are not published or are not available to the general public. In most cases, the author has worked directly with the researchers and many of these people are listed below. If you wish further information about a report or a project, it may be available by contacting the author or the report directly.

Without the generous help of many women who chose to speak out about rape to the author, much of the information in this book could not have been shared. Situations are modified in some case studies to protect the identity of the individual.

The author is especially grateful to Dr. Duncan Chappell, Director of the Law and Justice Study Center, Batelle Memorial Institute, Seattle, Washington and Dr. Johanna Shaw, Assistant Professor of Psychiatry, University of Vermont College of Medicine. These people read the manuscript in its entirety and supplied numerous helpful suggestions.

Interviews, personal letters, and suggestions of a wide variety came from people working at rape crisis centers, and from groups trying to change antiquated rape laws and outdated hospital procedures. Special thanks are due to:

Bay Area Women Against Rape, Berkeley, California

Bella Abzug, Member of Congress

Chicago Women Against Rape

Dr. Shirley Feldman-Summers, University of Washington, Seattle, Washington

Feminist Alliance Against Rape, Washington, D.C.

Lt. Mary Keefe, N.Y.C.P.D. Sex Crime Prevention Unit

Mary Ann Largen, Coordinator, National Rape Task Force, National Organization for Women

H. Rex Lewis, University of Chicago Hospitals and Clinics

Lynn O'Brien McLaughlin, Northern Vermont Chapter, National Organization for Women

William G. Milliken, Governor of Michigan

Montreal Rape Crisis Center, Montreal, Quebec

Nashville Rape Prevention and Crisis Center, Nashville, Tennessee

New York Women Against Rape, New York City

Dr. Joseph Peters, Center for Rape Concern, Philadelphia General Hospital

Dr. Gary F. Peterson, Hennepin County Medical Examiner, Minneapolis, Minnesota

Dr. Richard T. Rada, Associate Director of Research, University of New Mexico School of Medicine

Rape Crisis Center, Boston, Massachusetts

Rape Crisis Center, Madison, Wisconsin

Rape Crisis Center, P.O. Box 21005, Washington, D.C.

Rape Crisis Center, Women's Center, The University of New Mexico

Rape Crisis Line, Crisis Center of San Antonio Area, Inc., Texas

Rape Squad, Police Department, Chicago, Illinois

Santa Cruz Women Against Rape, Santa Cruz, California

South East Denver Neighborhood Service Crisis Line, Denver, Colorado

Springfield Rape Crisis Center, Springfield, Massachusetts

Task Force on Rape, Northern Vermont, NOW

University Women's Crisis Hotline, University of Maryland

Women Organized Against Rape, Philadelphia, Pennsylvania

Women Against Rape, Tri-Village Station, Columbus, Ohio

Women Against Rape, Detroit, Michigan

Women's Resource Center, Detroit, Michigan

SPEAK OUT ON RAPE!

Speaking Out About Rape

What is rape? What kind of people are rapists? Can you do something about this vicious form of assault? Can you help to stop rape? Why is rape a word that is heard so often these days? Why are people speaking out about rape?

Rape has many definitions, and the new meanings are different from the old. Although they vary from state to state, a common definition is: any sexual intimacy forced on one person by another. Rape is a violent assault committed through a sexual mode. Rape is defined broadly to include all sexual assaults, recognizing male as well as female victims. While problems encountered by children as well as adults of both sexes fall within the scope of rape by modern definitions, legal definitions in the past have excluded homosexual assaults, the rape of a wife, and a number of other kinds of sexual assaults.

Pioneers who first spoke about their rape experiences to other women and eventually to the world deserve much credit for bringing the violent crime of rape to the attention of today's society and for instigating changes in ancient and unjust laws. Some of the laws in the United States which deal with sex offenses have not been changed for almost 200 years.

Rape has thrived on silence, misunderstanding and prudery. Certainly the old attitude or myth, "Nice girls don't get raped and bad girls shouldn't complain," is partly responsible for the silence about this old and universal crime. The famous "Lord Hale instructions," which came down from the seventeenth century, required judges to give juries the information that rape is the easiest charge to make and the most difficult to prove. This and other antiquated practices which discriminate against a woman in court are undergoing change. According to a leading male authority in the legal field, an estimated two-thirds or more cases of rape are committed by offenders who are strangers to the victim. No wonder there is a national trend to view rape as a violent crime of assault rather than a deviant sexual offense or an act that is usually invited by women.

Concerned action by groups of young adults seem especially important in changing attitudes, and new laws suggest that people, both men and women, are *beginning* to change social attitudes about this crime and the sexism connected with it. The built-in skepticism toward women, which suggested that a female always provoked the attack, caused the suffering of many innocent women. The type of case in which a woman cried rape to vent her anger at a broken relationship with a man carried over, in some way, to every woman who was raped even though the victim had never seen her attacker before. If one was raped with a knife at her throat, she still had to prove her innocence in court.

Although the movement against rape seems almost explosive, there is much to be done beyond the present grass-root actions. Women far and wide are raising their voices, sharing ideas, and mobilizing against the crime of rape.

Venereal disease has been called "the silent epidemic," but perhaps the *most* silent tragedy is rape. Now the silence which has surrounded rape over the years is being infiltrated in many ways. For example, the newspaper of a small New England city carried the story of a rape of a fifteen-year-old girl in a shopping center at the north end of town. This was not the first time a girl had been raped there, nor was it the first time that the newspaper reported such an incident. But it was the first time the women in the neighborhood had talked about it in front of their young children. The next week "rape" was a word in a spelling bee.

"What does rape mean?" one eight-year-old asked another. "I think it's being attacked," answered one girl. "I think it means you have to go to the hospital to go to the bathroom," said another. No one was exactly sure, but all the children knew that rape was something to be avoided, and they all knew something about how to avoid it. Several years ago, when their older sisters were eight years old, no one spoke openly about rape. Many people then and many people today put the subject of rape out of their minds, somehow believing that by magical thinking the problem goes away.

For both young and old, rape has many meanings. Sometimes personal experience or knowledge about a friend's rape colors the meaning. But usually one turns to a dictionary. Here you find the following: "Rape is the crime of forcing a female to submit to sexual intercourse." "Rape is the act of seizing and carrying off by force or abduction." In this latter definition, there is no reference to sex. A third definition under the word rape in one dictionary is "abusive or improper treatment; violation; profanation; a rape of justice."

While fiction has dealt with the subject of rape for many centuries, if one looks for non-fiction books on rape related to sexual experiences, one finds only a short list and many of these are of recent date. There are many titles of books in print about rape other than sexual rape, such as *The Rape of the Masses, The Rape of Africa, The Rape of Art,* and *The Rape of the Lock.* Certainly, this does not mean that sexual rape is new, just that it has not been researched or discussed to any great extent.

No matter what the personal meaning, rape is a

problem which involves all of society; it occurs universally regardless of race or social class. Female human beings from the age of eight months to eighty years have been the victims of rape. City dwellers and rural dwellers are victims.

From cold climates to hot climates, from ancient times to recent times, people have been subject to sexual violence. At this very moment, you can be certain that someone is being raped. In short, rape is a problem which involves *everyone*. Although the rape victim is usually a female, her family and other loved ones as well as all of society suffer.

The Federal Bureau of Investigation in its Uniform Crime Report shows over 51,000 forcible rapes in one year. This is about a 70 percent rise over the figures released five years earlier. Some statistics on the rate of risk for females in large cities and in suburban areas are uncomfortably high, 18 percent of the females there are believed to have suffered rape. Actually, many authorities believe these statistics only represent the tip of an ominous iceberg, and the bulk of the number of such violent crimes lies hidden below the surface. Police reports to the F.B.I. may not even begin to measure the actual prevalence of rape throughout the U.S. While the reports indicate that forcible rape occurred in this country on the average of once every eleven minutes during a recent year, the true number is believed to be between four and ten times higher. There is probably one rape in the U.S. every minute, but problems which arise when a rape is reported deter many women from seeking help. Many of these problems are touched on throughout this book.

There are countless ways in which the threat of rape shapes the lives of girls and women. It may be that the only segment of the male population that best understands and experiences a fear comparable to that felt by all women is the men in prison who live, daily, with the threat of homosexual rape. Still, an increasing number of men are joining women in trying to prevent rape.

Why have the victims of rape remained silent? Why has this serious crime of assault on the body and the psyche been allowed to continue? Why are so few rapists actually convicted? The answers to these questions are complex.

While many individuals have sympathy for someone who has been raped, few can empathize or put themselves in the position of a person who has been so humiliated, injured, and violated. Relatively few people are *even aware* of the problems of the victim at the time of the rape and in the days, the months, and the years that follow.

While search for the truth about rape is just beginning, the large-scale social implications, the psychological problems of the victim and of the rapist are subjects of some recent research. With the rise in the reporting of rapes, and the suspicion that the victim risk-rate is rising, the subject is being brought from behind locked doors where it once was hidden—much the way emotionally disturbed children used to be hidden by their families. Many communities are examining the problems of prevention and control as well as the treatment and rehabilitation of rapists.

Rape is an issue which requires deeper and broader understanding. The questions about it are many and varied. They are questions that need answers from more people than just the rape victims and their families. From the frightened woman who walks alone in a quiet place, and the mangled victim of rape lying in a hospital bed, to the victimized woman who sits on the witness stand during a legal trial—in which she is actually the witness for the prosecution but treated like the defendant—much remains to be learned and changed. For the innocent little girl in her playpen, for the old woman alone in her apartment, for women and for men of all ages, the prevention of rape is a subject of major importance. Coping with the idea of rape, exploding the myths, education about prevention, what to do in the case of rape, and how to help those who experience rape are explored to some degree in the following pages.

Who Is the Rapist?

If you raise the question, "What kind of people are rapists?" before a large group, you would probably find that there are a number of common ideas, but that many of the ideas are myths. For example, large numbers of people believe that black men are more likely to attack white women than they are likely to attack black women. Many people believe that poor men typically attack rich women. Yet studies show that the rapist and his victim tend to be of the same race and class. According to the leading study by Menachem Amir, *Patterns in Forcible Rape*, 77 percent of all rapes have been committed by black men raping black women. However, white women who have been raped by black men have received so much widespread support in most cases, that the ensuing publicity may be responsible for this racist myth.

Myths abound, partly because there is so little research on the subject, partly because of the lack of education and easily available information, and partly because each rape case is different from every other one. From many areas of study on the subject of rape have come somewhat conflicting conclusions. One of the few subjects on which there is considerable agreement is the age of the rapist. While most offenders go undetected, the reported rapes indicate the most common age group for offenders to be the same as that of the most crime-prone group of males—those between the ages of fifteen and twenty-four years.

According to Dr. John MacDonald of the University of Colorado Medical Center, almost 50 percent of the offenders in a study of 232 Denver rapists were between the ages of fifteen and twenty-five. Almost 75 percent of them were below thirty years of age. He reports that the median age for offenders in Philadelphia was twenty-three, and only 14 percent were over thirty years of age.

Many people believe that relatively few rapists are married, but actually the percentage of married rapists is high. In one survey, 40 percent were married, 13 percent were divorced, and 43 percent were single. Recent studies in three different counties each report that between 40 percent and 43 percent of the rapists are married. Rape is considered as a planned crime rather than an impulsive act in a great majority of cases.

While many feminist groups consider every man a potential rapist, with this kind of action programmed in him because of society's treatment of women, there are many theories about the kind of man who actually commits the crime of rape. What is the difference between the man who rapes and the man who does not? Is the rapist really "the man next door"? He may, in some cases, be just that, but why does one man behave criminally while another does not? How much is sociocultural? How much is biology or chemistry? Is genetics involved? For example, according to one theory, a rapist may be a loner who acts out his problems in a criminal way. He may be a friend of the victim or a relative who in all other respects appears to live a normally adjusted life. These men seem normal, yet they suffer from character disorders which lead them to commit sex offenses. Criminologists do not know how much these factors, or which of these factors, "compel" a man to behave as a rapist. There are no easy or pat answers. Certainly, it is evident that more knowledge is needed concerning the real cause of rape.

According to researchers at the Institute for Sex Research at Indiana University, the behavior of rapists tends to develop individually, and is not learned from others. Although most rapes are carried out by individuals and independently of other men, reports nevertheless show a good deal of similarity in the conduct and the reaction of rapists when questioned about their behavior. A surprising number of rapists felt that the girl enjoyed the situation. If there was a lack of physical struggle, they interpreted this as cooperation. A threat of death, a paralyzing fear on the part of the woman, a remark that the woman would not be hurt if she cooperated were easily forgotten by the rapist. A surprising number of rapists who believed that the victim really enjoyed the rape agreed with the girl's request to return for a second visit and in this way were trapped by police, who were alerted by the victim.

Little is really known about classifications of rapists and some reports are conflicting, but attempts have been made to group them. Some follow: one kind of rapist, whose prime motivation is sex, feels extremely insecure and is simply acting out his fantasy. He is unable to have a normal sex life, but by raping a woman he no longer feels weak and inferior. Such men are not sadistic, they simply have a sexual urge and do not care about the feelings or wishes of the female, whom they consider to be objects whose role in life is to provide sexual pleasure. According to some authorities, these men are making an effort to suppress homosexual feelings. Others, who consider homosexuality as normal, believe that this idea is totally unfounded, for it considers rapists to be repressed homosexuals and implies that such men are sick and capable of sexually motivated rape. But those who consider the study valid observe that this type of rapist, who is characteristically a man acting out fantasies, is one who easily becomes frightened by women who resist his advances.

Another kind of rapist, who is an amoral delinquent, has no feelings about right or wrong. This type is sadistic and responsible for some of the most brutal sexual acts. He may unconsciously consider women as pleasantly shaped masses of protoplasm for sexual use. Such men pay little heed to any social control and operate through a desire for their own self-pleasure. They usually have had many brushes with the law, for they take what they want, be it property, such as a television set, or a human body.

One variety of rape is committed by a man who is not gratified by the sexual experience alone but also must include physical violence or the threat of it. A sadistic rapist does not get the same thrill from the rape if the victim does not resist. This kind of behavior sometimes occurs when the victim remains passive and does not respond physically during the act. In one report, an eighty-five-year-old woman reported that a man tried to kill her and kept hitting her time and time again. He asked where she hid her money, he tried to rape her, to choke her, and tear off her clothes. He ransacked the house after the old woman got away. She knocked on her neighbor's door and was admitted there. At first she could not talk for having been choked, but her neighbor immediately called the police.

The saying, "If you are going to rob a woman, you might as well rape her. The rape is free," brings up the connection between rape and burglary. Rapists *sometimes* use the idea of setting a mind at ease by saying that all they want is a girl's money. They feel this may put her off her guard. On the other hand, many steal from their victims after the act of rape, taking valuable articles which are available. Opportunist rapes are not uncommon. A burglar who finds a woman in an apartment often decides to add rape to the burglary.

The question of how many physical threats are actually carried out is a difficult one to answer. Sometimes an offender runs away when a woman screams or physically attacks him. However, his threat *may* be carried out if she attempts to resist. Each case seems different and there is no hard-and-fast rule as to what a rapist will do. While some rapists claim to have a weapon and do not produce it, other do show their knives, guns, or iron bars. A number make use of weapons even to the extent of killing the victim. In some cases, reports indicate, a rapist compares this rape assault with other rape experiences in which he knocked out teeth, cut a victim or tortured a girl.

Many rapists are grouped together as having a double standard. These men divide women into one group whom they treat with respect and another group whom they feel entitled to rape since they judge them to be sexually promiscuous. These men tend to indulge in group activity and several are apt to cruise about in a car looking for girls to pick up. They share a girl much as they would share food or liquor. Such men may share their pickups with other men but insist on fidelity from their wives or from the woman they intend to marry.

Another kind of rapist is called the explosive variety. This type is believed to constitute about 10 percent to 15 percent of all offenders, according to some studies. Bill is typical of this kind of rapist. He is mild, a straight-A student who is obedient and hard working. He seems to be respectful toward authority, have a sense of personal responsibility, family pride, and many other fine traits. Bill knows the difference between right and wrong and is willing to abide by these differences, but beneath the surface his anxieties and hostilities remain bottled up. Recently, it has been noted that he worries a great deal and becomes emotionally upset easily. Still, when Bill's exemplary behavior falls apart it is totally unexpected. It happens suddenly. He notes that the door of the apartment down the hall from his is open and he enters, hears the shower running, and visualizes the pretty young girl who lives there standing nude in the shower. As Bill bumps against a table, she hears the noise, throws a towel around herself, and moves to investigate. As Bill comes close to her, his hostility explodes and he throws the young woman on the bed nearby. The girl's dog barks and nips at him. Bill seems to be the neighbor out of character. He is the rapist whose fantasies and hostilities can no longer be contained in the straight but "uptight" personality he has worn so long as a mask.

Many feminists feel that a general reason for rape is

hostility against women. Such a rapist may be brutal, although violence is not necessarily a part of the crime. The humiliation of the victim may be enough to satisfy his pent-up emotions of rage, contempt, and hatred against women in general. For him, rape is a form of hostility and aggression, and is seen as the ultimate act of attacking a woman as an animal, rather than considering her as a person. The victim of the rape is not necessarily the object of the rapist's wrath. In certain cases, a man may attack any female as representing one particular woman who rejected him, such as his mother or a lover.

The least aggressive type of rapist is one who is drunk. In some cases, the intoxication provides an outlet for underlying hostile impulses, but this is not always the case. In his report of the following drunken offenses, the male author, Dr. John MacDonald in *Rape: Offenders and Their Victims,* describes them as relatively harmless. The victim undoubtedly would disagree. The man on two occasions had forced himself on women who yielded in order to get it over with and get rid of him. He probably felt that minor force was safe and effective in obtaining what he wanted from a woman, so he did not anticipate trouble. On a third occasion when he had been drinking, he peeked in a window of a motel room and saw a young woman asleep. He thought of crawling into bed with her and he broke the window screen. Being intoxicated, he was not concerned with being caught in an illegal act. Then he remembered that he was not properly clothed for bed, so he went to his own motel room and changed into his pajamas. He then went back to the girl's room, removed the broken screen from the window and crawled into bed with her. The girl awoke and screamed, so he clapped his hands over her mouth. She became quiet, perhaps because she fainted. The attacker removed his hand from her mouth in order to kiss her and at that the girl began to scream again and scratch. At this point, the attacker, severely scratched, stumbled to the door and fell into the grasp of a man who had been attracted by the screams of the victim. Thus, it is obvious that even in its most "innocuous" form, rape is an ugly offense.

According to a recent report on alcoholic customs in sexual life, it was noted that alcohol releases the ordinarily unconscious desire to commit rape, incest, sex murders and other violent sexual offenses. Therefore, the struggle against alcoholism is also a struggle against the negative aspects of sexual life.

Alcohol and drugs play a significant part in group rapes, which are becoming more common each day. These are rapes in which the victim is attacked by two to five men. Sometimes one of the men holds the victim while the others watch. Many times an individual offender will threaten to turn his friends on his victim if she does not cooperate with him.

Rapes in which from five to twenty take part are called "gang" rapes and they are a feature of the social life of street gangs in larger cities. Some authorities believe that gang rape and the spontaneous rituals of gang behavior arise because of the culture's refusal to meet adolescents' needs during a critical period. Gang rapes take on many of the characteristics of such cultural rituals as the puberty rite. Group rape, in which fewer than five take part, seem to reveal roots in immature psychosexual development and combines aggressive and sexual drives with exhibitionistic tendencies, homosexual fears, and castration anxieties.

Gang or "pack rapes" are described by G. D. Woods in the Australian and New Zealand Journal of Criminology. In a United States government synopsis of the report one finds the following information about pack rape in certain Sydney, Australia suburbs: its occurrence can be related to both population increase and consequent social disorganization. The propinquity of open land facilitates the commission of the crime, as does the availability of motor cars in the sixteen-to-twenty age group. It is primarily a group offense committed by delinquent gangs. The members of these gangs are accustomed to group sexual intercourse with girls who seek a kind of acceptance in the gang which they fail to find elsewhere. It is extremely difficult to distinguish situations where there has been consent from situations where there has been none. The report recommends that social and judicial reactions to this offense ought not be overly punitive, and rejects, in particular, suggestions that offenders be hanged, whipped or castrated. There would seem to be no alternative to jail sentences, but because the crime is a group one, sentences need only be long enough to ensure that the particular group will have broken up by the time the offender is released, according to the report. Most women who read this synopsis will tend to believe that the author is a man.

Just a few of the ways rapists are seen by various authorities have been described here. Most feminist groups and many researchers believe that the rapist is not emotionally sick and that the prevention of rape depends on changing sexist attitudes in the whole social structure of today's world. According to them, it is only when the conditions which produce the male-dominated society and the justice system are changed, that rape can be prevented.

Some men agree with the feminists, even some who were rapists. In an article in a recent issue of *Feminist Alliance Against Rape Newsletter,* a group known as Prisoners Against Rape state their case. They believe that rape, like other crimes, grows out of social environment and that rape is a product of the racist and repressive ills tied into the American way of life, a way which is ingrained into the masses from the cradle. In the article, the founders of Prisoners Against Rape quote: "Have we, perhaps, been focusing our attention on the wrong part of the problem—on the offender and his mental condition instead of on the conditions which produced him?" These words are quoted from David L. Bazelon, Chief Judge of the United States Court of Appeals for the District of Columbia Circuit.

Who is the rapist? Is he the product of society? Is he a normal man suffering from a temporary disease?

Certainly little is known about the rapist. While some authorities try to categorize types of rapists, many others search for causes and prevention. With women spearheading the movement, rape has become a national issue of considerable concern, and the expanded research may throw more light on *who is a rapist?*

The Rape Victim: from Childhood to Old Age

Females are the vulnerable victims of rape from the cradle to the last years of their lives. Although rape is a common, violent crime, the victims of rape appear to the great majority of people as vague statistics mentioned briefly in newspaper reports. A rape victim may be the woman next door, but if she is, it is doubtful that she will let you know about her misfortune, whether it happened long in the past or recently. You may have several friends who have been the victims of rape, but since this crime usually makes the victim appear to be guilty, even close friends may not tell. Many women prefer to keep the experience entirely to themselves or to confide only in a family doctor, one family member, or one friend.

As the subject of rape gains attention, the problems confronting its victims are becoming problems of a more aware society. High school guidance counselors are beginning to recognize that some of their students have had to deal with rape. They acknowledge the fact that almost all girls will be able to cope better if they are aware of the problem and have been alerted about how to prevent rape, coping with a rapist, and how to obtain help afterward. Some pre-rape education is being introduced as a result of peer pressure.

On the other hand, a victim of rape may be treated with unbelievable cruelty by her classmates. For example, a fifteen-year-old high school student who was recently raped while walking to school received anonymous and obscene notes from classmates for a period of several weeks after the incident. The rape of a fifteen-year-old, or of any minor, is classed as statutory rape on the basis that the girl or boy was not old enough to give informed consent to the person who committed the assault.

Statutory rape need not be forcible rape. Incest has a different meaning. Incest is defined as sexual intercourse between relatives with the closeness of the relationship usually being defined by law as closer than first cousins. In many cases of statutory rape, the victim is a young child who knows the rapist and even loves him, for he may be a close family friend.

So far, in this book, the rapist has generally been considered to be a male and the victim has been considered to be a female. Although this is almost always the case, males, under special circumstances, are subject to rape or sexual assault too. On rare occasions, females help males to rape members of their own sex. Rape may be charged of those women who act as accomplices. In one case, a female was raped by three men after she was enticed into a bedroom by another woman.

Actual sexual assault of women upon men is recorded to be a practice among a tribe in South America, known as the Kogi. Women in groups of two or three have the customary right to attack a passerby from another village. Such a man is fair game for any sexual abuse the women care to practice on him.

Many cases of seduction of young boys by women may occur but few are reported in any way. One case that came to the notice of authorities was that of a woman in India who seduced five boys ranging from ten to fourteen years of age. It is thought that she believed intercourse with a child would rid her of venereal disease!

While a case of a woman seducing a young boy rarely comes before the courts, much of the same is true of cases where children are involved in other kinds of sex offenses. According to one survey of child sex abuse, 75 percent of the offenders were known to the child victim and/or the child's family. Of these, most of the offenders were males between the ages of seventeen and sixty-eight, and 27 percent of these were members of the child's household. Eleven percent of the child victims were related to the offenders. In this study, the children were between infancy and sixteen years of age with the median age being 11.2 years. For every boy victim, there were ten girls. Most of the boys were involved in homosexual activity.

Would you expect parents to come to the defense of their children if they knew about their sexual abuse? Only about half of the children who are known victims of sex offenses appear to tell their parents or other people about them immediately after they happen or within one day of the abuse. Considering the traumatic quality of such an experience, one might expect parents to be greatly concerned. But in some cases, the experience appears to be much more traumatic for the parent than for the child and their reactions may surprise you. For example, in 173 cases in which child victims of sexual offense were brought into court, the children were involved in over 1,000 court appearances. However, fewer than 33 percent of the parents prosecuted out of concern for the child or to protect the child from further abuse. In some of the prosecutions, the orientation was toward protecting the offender. If parents side with the offender, a child might be more seriously injured emotionally than by the physical injury of the sexual offense.

Consider the following kind of experience, which is not rare. A young girl is left with a baby-sitter—a teenage boy—evening after evening. After she is raped, she reports the incident to her mother. The chief concern of the mother may not be for the child but for herself. The sitter's mother and the child's mother are friends. If she tells the boy's mother, her friendship will be ruined. If she tells her husband, he will complain of the irresponsible way she selected a sitter. So instead of protecting the child or even appreciating the child's feelings, the mother protects herself. She persuades the child to think that her father could suffer a heart attack if the incident were revealed, and the future of the boy could be ruined. The girl, who loves her father and likes the sitter, respects her mother's wishes but suffers emotional damage which interferes with her personality development, especially in her future relationships with men. And since her mother has not come to her defense, the guilt feelings of the mother are adopted by the child. When she matures, acute anxiety interferes with sexual attractions and she is unable to form serious attachments to men.

The psychological upset to the child that follows rape may damage a child's personality, especially when the child is used to prosecute the offender. Since evidence suggests that children can quickly adjust to the situation after an offense if parents do not emphasize guilt, help from professionals can be especially important. Many well-intentioned parents add to the injury when they have no guidance in such situations. A social worker may help parents cope with the problem, especially if they need to prove to themselves and society that the child did not participate voluntarily. Such participation would make them feel they had failed in their role as parents.

Some adults contend that children provoke rape and are not just innocent bystanders. Although children are sexual persons and may appear to invite sexual relations, their provocation is *childish* fantasy appropriate to their age. The adult has adult sexual interests and responsibilities, so he or she is completely responsible for abuse or perversion.

Many children and adults, too, never report sexual abuse because they have been threatened by the offender. This may be a stepfather, an uncle, a father, or a friend of the father's, and the child may either fear disbelief or further abuse. When women began speaking out about rape, many told of being raped as a child or of being abused sexually in other ways by adults whom they knew. Women also recalled the fears they experienced that prevented their telling anyone at the time of the occurrence. Through the current freedom from fear in which women share their experiences that are buried in their minds from years ago, one finds that child rape is not as rare as one might suppose.

While most child abuse continues unreported, Women Organized Against Rape (WOAR) in Philadelphia, report that 40 percent of the victims which they see are between the ages of eighteen months and sixteen years, and that 65 percent of all victims seen are under twenty years of age. How can such young children and young women be helped to cope with such a traumatic experience? One way would be to reform juvenile justice systems. Some action is being taken here, but more support from individual citizens is needed.

In many communities, money is spent freely to convict the rapist. In some, money is spent in an attempt to rehabilitate the offender. But little is done to help the victim. In fact, the criminal justice system, through its outdated court procedures, may hurt the victim even more than the rapist, who usually goes free. Although the unpleasant and sometimes almost vicious treatment of the victim in court may be unintentional or just a part of the rapist's defense, it is nonetheless real to the person who has already suffered the traumatic experience of rape.

According to group studies, children complain less of physical problems than adults after sexual abuse. This may be partly due to the fact that child sex offenses are often grouped so that rape, exhibitionism, and other sex abuses are not considered separately. Another reason may be that the child victim often knows the offender and may not be harmed physically. But the study of individual children shows they suffer some very traumatic effects.

Consider the case of a father who was convicted of having intercourse with his nine-year-old and sixteen-year-old daughters. Although he had been to court, he was excused from the regular group therapy program, which was established in his locality for men with such problems, because he preferred individual therapy. The judge agreed to private treatment, but during the probationary period, this man continued to have intercourse with his daughters until they reported this fact to their mother. At one point in the court trial of the father, the older daughter was called upon to identify a film which her father had made of them having sexual relations. The father was sentenced to five years in prison, but the mother thought the sentence too short. The girl, who was the victim of the court trial as well as the father's mistreatment, felt guilty because she had played a part in her father's imprisonment. She also felt guilty about her sexual relationship with her father. Her mother's attitude entered into the picture, too, since the mother wanted to open the court case again in order to try to get a longer sentence for her husband. How did this affect the victim? What were the daughter's feelings about her mother's willingness to expose her once more to the court proceedings and to the sex film? This young girl had good reason to be in a state of turmoil.

Children, as stated earlier, may be accused of victim-precipitated rape, but there is more sympathy for them than the women accused of being victims who "asked for it." Many judges and men who study the problem of rape feel that some women are "rape prone" just as some people are "accident prone." Many do seem to be oblivious to danger signs or warnings and make themselves easy victims, whether consciously or unconsciously. Education may help these people to avoid becoming victims. Ways of preventing rape, which are discussed in a later chapter, may be unknown to women who court potential offenders without assessing the danger. The comparatively few women who are guilty of false rape accusations have made it difficult for the many women who are innocent victims.

A potential rapist looks for a victim that is vulnerable to attack. For example, he may drive alongside a car in which a woman is driving alone and call to her for directions, warn her of a flat tire, or use any excuse to test her reaction. Although there is no proof, some people who work with rape victims feel that a woman who appears friendly or anxious is more likely to become a victim that one who remains aloof and cool in manner.

Women's groups who are forming to fight rape insist that a woman should be allowed to dress any way she wishes and that "seductive" behavior or dress should play no part in determining the guilt of the rapist. Sociologists do not all agree with this approach, and consider a rape victim-precipitated if a girl behaves in a manner that leads a man to believe that she is willing to have sexual relations. The women's groups say that a person who waves money while walking along the street and is attacked by a mugger is not considered guilty. Why, then, should the behavior or dress of a woman count against her when she becomes the victim of rape?

No matter how much disagreement there is on the subject of victim-precipitated rape, few disagree with the fact that certain conditions make some women more prone to be raped than others. The lonesome person who is flattered by the attention of the rapist looking for a victim is more vulnerable than a woman who ignores any questions or comments from a strange man. The woman who is intoxicated is easy prey. Handicapped women who cannot react quickly to the threat of rape are especially vulnerable. Men sometimes rape women who hitchhike. "Sisters Pick Up Sisters" has become a motto among many women who must hitchhike because other transportation is unavailable. The list of victims and problems resulting from hitchhiking is long and varied.

In some areas more than half the reported cases of rape occur when the victim is a complete stranger to the rapist. In New York City, the estimate is 70 percent; Denver and Seattle report 65 percent of their rapes are between total strangers. Although she may be chosen in advance of the incident, the victim may be completely unaware that the man exists. Some rapists watch the pattern of a woman's activities for several days. Others seek out places relatively safe from intrusion, such as laundry rooms at night, apartment basement halls that are rarely used, and isolated rest rooms. Women who frequent such areas run a greater risk of being raped than those who avoid them.

According to one estimate, a woman's chances of becoming a rape victim in some cities may be as great as one in ten over a thirty-year period. Even if this is exaggerated, rape remains a serious threat. No wonder many women and some men are striking out against this common and horrible crime which victimizes a woman in so many ways. Hopefully, they will succeed to the degree that a woman can walk alone without fear in a dark hall or a silent woods, where she may know peace, beauty, and quiet, in safety.

Medical Help Immediately after Rape

Any rape victim suffers psychologically. The damage varies in degree and time, and it has many patterns. Briefly, there is the acute stage of disbelief and shock during and immediately after the assault. At this time, a woman continues to tell herself that "this is not happening to me," and there is an overwhelming sense of helplessness. The second stage, which comes after a varying amount of time has passed, is an outwardly adjusted stage. The victim seems to have coped with the problem and may feel that it will never bother her again. The third stage is one of depression, irritability, and anger. These reactions will be discussed in more detail.

Immediately after the rape, many victims need emergency hospital care because of physical injuries, about 20 percent, according to one study. These vary from minor scratches and bruises to open heart sur-

gery. Because of the possibility of pregnancy and
venereal disease, all victims should have medical care
even though they are not suffering from physical
wounds. Many women who are raped, however, have a
strong denial syndrome—they refuse to accept the fact
that they have been raped. For this reason, they wait
many hours or days before becoming concerned about
pregnancy and VD. Then they become aware of such
dangers and seek medical help. Some people are
afraid that public attention will be focused on them if
they obtain medical care, so they *never* consult a doctor
but suffer in silence. This is unfortunate, for medical
care of good quality should be available, and every
woman should know what to do in case of rape.

Consider the case of Linda, who had never given
any thought to the idea that she might be raped. Linda
was raped when she went to the garbage disposal area
of her apartment building. She felt a hand on her wrist
and she heard a voice from behind her saying, "Don't
scream, I am armed." There was no one in sight as
Linda faced the overflow of trash near the incinerator.
She was afraid to turn or cry for help. Suddenly, the
man seemed to melt into the surroundings and Linda
lost consciousness.

After Linda became conscious again and realized
she had been raped, she felt some relief that she had
survived. She knew that she was physically hurt and
had to reach a doctor. She also felt an intense need to
wipe out the experience, to go to the shower, to tear up
her clothing and destroy all evidence of what had

happened. She also wanted to talk to someone who would be sympathetic to her problem. A neighbor discovered Linda in hysterics, still lying on the floor.

The neighbor took Linda to the nearest hospital emergency ward, then left her to tend to some problems at home. This hospital emergency room was set up to take care of physical emergencies such as broken bones, heart attacks, serious cuts and skull injuries. Linda was not bleeding or in danger of dying, and her bruises were not extensive, so she had to wait. One of the doctors in the hospital had had some experience treating so-called "professional" rape victims, women who had accused men of rape because of their personal anger against them. Although professional victims appear to be in the great minority, many doctors seem to be able to feel more empathy for men than for helpless victims of rape. Other doctors are unsympathetic because they wish to avoid the court involvement which may follow the examination of a rape victim. Such doctors are in no hurry to treat victims like Linda.

Studies also show that immediately after rape, a victim is particularly sensitive to the attitude of the people around her. In the hospital, no one seemed to care about Linda's experience. She did not realize they were very busy with people who had more serious medical problems. Linda felt neglected, embarrassed, and ashamed while she waited for treatment. She was asked to fill out a number of forms. In addition to the usual information asked by hospital people when one goes to an emergency room for treatment, Linda was asked to sign consent for the following: examinations, the collection of specimens, the taking of photographs, and the releasing of information to proper authorities. This was to allow the doctor to collect evidence which would help her if she decided to prosecute the rapist. No one explained to Linda why she had to fill out all these forms, nor did anyone seem to understand that she was very disturbed by the terrible emotional experience she had just had. She sat alone in the waiting room of the hospital's emergency ward for several hours. Linda did not look at her watch. She did not look at the people around her. She was just trying to cope with her sense of helplessness.

While Linda was waiting, she began to wonder why she had not fought back when she was attacked. Could she have escaped from the man? But then she wondered if fighting back might have meant her life, for an armed rapist can and does kill victims in some cases. At that point in time, Linda's first concern was her survival.

Hours went by. Linda was taken to an examination room where a doctor treated her rather bruskly, and made her feel uncomfortable, almost guilty for having been the victim of rape. Although he took the tests which are standard procedure following sexual assault, such as those which could be used in court to verify the rape and those which are necessary to protect the well-being of the victim, he never explained this procedure. Unfortunately, the necessary questions made Linda relive the horrible experience and increased her sense of anxiety and sense of embarrassment and helplessness.

The doctor's questions about possible pregnancy were made only to protect Linda from such a condition. She felt, however, that he was prying into her private life by asking about her use of birth control pills. Actually, he would have told her what options she had if she had not been protected by her pills.

Linda had not considered the possibility of venereal disease from the contact with the rapist. When the doctor gave her a preventive injection of penicillin she was shocked when he suggested that she have further checks to make certain that she had not contracted a venereal disease. He told her not to worry—she could not be pregnant, she would not get VD, and she was not seriously injured—she might just as well forget about the incident. Just like that—forget it! But her whole world had been shattered.

The medical treatment which Linda received did not help her to cope with the emotional problems that many women have after such a traumatic experience. Some of these are apparent at the acute stage, immediately after the attack. Many psychiatrists feel that immediate and sympathetic medical care can do much to lessen the problems that can develop afterward.

Women who have been raped usually appreciate someone who will listen sympathetically and objectively without a judgmental attitude. Unfortunately, at many medical examinations there is some tendency to focus attention on whether or not a woman was really raped. If the victim is calm, or appears calm, and has no signs of physical injury, this may be held against her in legal procedures.

Better medical care is one of the reasons that women have organized against rape, and the movement is growing rapidly. There are services available to many urban women at time of crisis, and women in towns and rural areas are also forming groups to help rape victims. A variety of types of help are becoming available. Not the least of these is help immediately after the assault. Many recent victims report that their experience has been less tragic as a result of their knowledge of a rape crisis hotline.

If a rape victim calls a hotline number of a rape crisis center, a volunteer may be sent at once to the scene of the rape, or wherever the woman may be. This volunteer is trained to help the victim. Her supportive care begins immediately and if it is accepted, continues for a long period of time. Such a volunteer may take the first step to help the rape victim by providing transportation from the scene of the rape to a doctor's office or the emergency room of a cooperative hospital.

Not all hospitals or clinics welcome rape victims and some even refuse to cooperate. According to one report, a university hospital tried to shield one of its students from publicity after she had been raped in a dormitory building. The staff even withheld information about the incident from authorities in order to prevent further panic among other students, since the number of recent rapes was causing increasing concern around campus. A persistent reporter uncovered the incident and hospital staff members were severely censured even though they claimed their intentions were to shield the victim. This university hospital no longer accepts rape victims but sends them to the large city hospital for examination and treatment.

In an effort to help both medical staffs and the women who are the victims of rape, the Task Force on Rape of the Women's Equity Action League (WEAL) has recommended that a number of gynecologists participate in publically-funded programs to treat rape victims, that they be knowledgeable about court proceedings, and be prepared to testify in court. This would eliminate many examining physicians' fears of becoming involved, because they would no longer have to take time off to be present in a court case. It could prevent inadequate treatment of a victim by a doctor who is not familiar with procedures, and avoid contact with unsympathetic doctors who have the attitude that a raped woman may have "asked for it."

A volunteer from a rape crisis center knows where a rape victim will receive sympathetic care and the proper medical treatment. She is also aware of how specimens must be handled if they are to be used as legal evidence at a later date.

A worker from a rape crisis center may be able to guide a victim to a hospital where she will receive understanding treatment. She can explain that *some* hospitals are knowledgeable about treating rape patients. Nurses and counselors may provide information about how other women who have been raped feel afterward. They counsel victims by making them aware that many women have similar feelings after such a traumatic experience. The victims are not abnormal in their reactions of feeling isolated, alienated, and very concerned about their own and loved ones' responses to the situation. Some women report a general feeling of soreness all over their bodies and many victims have difficulty with sleeping patterns and nightmares. Unfortunately, many hospitals do not have staff members who can counsel rape victims in the emergency room, and in some instances staff members may seem, or even be, hostile to a rape victim.

One of the questions which a worker from a rape crisis center can answer is why the rape victim may seem to be pushed aside in the emergency room. She can explain the hospital system used to decide which patient should be treated first. If one's physical injury is minor, he or she would have to wait for a person with a severe emergency to be treated first, even if such a person arrived later. This assignment of low priority is sometimes hard to understand, and a rape victim may well feel that no case can be more important than hers.

What about venereal disease? A rape crisis worker can explain that penicillin which is given at the first medical examination is a preventive measure, but that the presence of syphilis cannot be diagnosed immediately after the rape. It is important for the rape victim to report for blood tests five or six weeks later. If the tests are positive, penicillin or other drugs can be used to cure the syphilis. In the case of gonorrhea, an even more common venereal disease, smears are taken at the first pelvic examination. Results of any positive tests are relayed to the rape victim so she can obtain proper medication and can prevent the physical damage caused by this disease. Venereal diseases can be cured, and the tests which reveal their presence are readily available.

While in the waiting room, a rape victim may begin to wonder if she might become pregnant as a result of the rape. A trained worker from a rape crisis center could comfort the victim by giving her information on this matter, and by informing her of the options she has available. It would undoubtedly comfort a rape victim to know that a menstrual period is often late after rape because of emotional stress. And for those women who wish to terminate pregnancy or possible pregnancy, there are several options. One is "the morning after pill," usually stilbestrol (DES). This is given in large doses and can be administered either as a single injection or as a series of pills to be taken twice a day for a period of five days. The injection should be given within twenty-four hours of the rape. If the pills are preferred, they should be started within the same period of time. All of the pills must be taken in order for them to be effective. Unfortunately, the "morning after pill" is considered dangerous for some women, especially those who have any of a number of diseases such as high blood pressure, a family history of poor blood clotting, sickle-cell anemia, sickle-cell trait, or cancer. It may be particularly dangerous for a woman whose mother took stilbestrol before she was born. Some women experience side effects from taking stilbestrol, such as stomachaches, headaches, vomiting and dizziness.

Some rape victims prefer to wait until an accurate pregnancy test can be made two weeks after a menstrual period is missed. In some cases, pregnant women may menstruate at the normal time and this may be misleading. Many doctors recommend a pregnancy test for all women who are not practicing birth control, especially if they are raped about the fourteenth day of their cycle.

If a woman's pregnancy test is positive she may wish to have an abortion. In such a case, it is best to make arrangements as soon as possible, for an early abortion is the safest and easiest.

For legal purposes, pubic hair, any foreign fiber or bloodstains on the victim's clothing, and any seminal fluid from the genital area are sent to the laboratory. The blood type of about 80 percent of men can be identified from their seminal fluid. If the victim decides that she wants to prosecute, these will be available. A woman may not know at the time of the examination what she wants to do but many doctors collect such specimens routinely. Doctors who have worked with rape victims in court know that these specimens must be labeled permanently and clearly. They etch slides with a diamond pencil and indicate the patient's name and the date on them.

Sometimes legal evidence taken at the time of a medical examination is inadmissable because it is not transferred from one individual to another through the proper chain of custody. Evidence should be sealed in a locked box and handled by security men or physicians at a hospital. The key of the box should be transferred through as few hands as possible until laboratory testing is complete. Since any person who has had the key in his or her possession while the material was in the box, is a potential court witness, it is obvious that the number of persons involved should be minimal.

An accurate and systematic laboratory examination is an important part of the total care of the rape victim. Guiding a woman to a doctor who is familiar with procedures and sympathetic to the problem of rape is a very important function of a rape crisis center. If specimens are collected, tested, handled, and interpreted carefully, the rape victim, the physician, and all of society will benefit.

Legal Aspects of Rape

Perhaps no area of the social disease known as rape is more shrouded with myths and antiquated ideas than the legal aspects. Here many of the laws are based on ancient attitudes and the way in which they are administered helps to protect the rapist rather than the victim. She may be treated as a criminal even though she had never before seen the man who assaulted her. Women have been viewed as asking to be victimized in a great many cases. This is especially true for young, attractive women. No matter what the circumstances of the rape, women have long been confronted by laws designed to protect the rapist. These laws may still assume that the woman is protected by her husband or father, since she was considered their property in the days when the laws were made. And if such is the case, the crime is one of man against man, of the protection of male property rights.

Rape victims who take their cases to court are often made to feel that they are on trial instead of the accused. "And I thought the rape was bad," is a common response after a trial. Again and again, women who have gone to court suffered intense emotional experiences as the result of a defense attorney's accusations about her character and actions. In some states, women may suffer by having their past sexual involvements exposed, although they have no connection with the rape. In spite of the victims' ordeals and attempts to obtain some justice in court, the majority of the accused rapists go free.

It is not surprising to find the changing of laws relating to forcible rape in the vanguard of those issues affecting women's rights. The criminal justice system is now being forced to reappraise its approach to this crime because of social and political pressures.

Men, as well as women, are becoming more and more convinced that a rational code of sex offense laws is long overdue. According to a recent study by Morris Ploscowe, titled "Sex Offenses: The American Legal Content," sex offense legislation presently on the books is largely unenforceable and much of it does a great deal more harm than good. He suggests a number of fundamental reasons for this situation, including the fact that prohibitions for sex offenses are far too inclusive, covering many areas of behavior.

Laws and literature about rape have been so dominated by fear of falsely convicting an innocent man that the rapists have long been on a "winning streak"!

Certainly the legal framework should not appear to place the woman on trial, no matter how aware both men and women may be of the fact that false conviction is just as harmful as false acquittal. More and more prosecutors and judges are acknowledging that present rape laws combine myth with reality, and are helping to change them so that they are not the ally of the rapist.

Although rape has long been treated differently from other crimes, new and fairer rape laws are appearing in *many* places across the United States. For example, a number of states now prohibit, in the prosecution for rape, use of the victim's past sexual history with men other than the accused.

A number of states have changed, or are in the process of changing, some of their rules of evidence to limit the introduction, in a trial, of material about a victim's personal sex life, except in limited instances. New York, Colorado, California, Texas, Minnesota, Oregon, Iowa, Nevada, New Mexico, Nebraska, and Michigan have enacted such legislation. Many other states are in the process of proposing or passing laws which help to eliminate demeaning cross-examination. Revisions throughout the country aim to encourage more women to seek police help, so that more rapists can be arrested and prosecutors can increase the rate of convictions.

Corroboration, which is physical evidence of the rape attempt, and evidence of the victim's lack of consent, is still considered important in some states. A victim's testimony might have to be substantiated by the testimony of others. She might be asked to prove lack of consent, use of force, penetration, severe injuries, and even provide eyewitness testimony. One wonders how a victim who is experiencing sexual assault could ever provide eyewitness testimony. Feminists and others find such aspects of the law heavily weighted in favor of the rapist. Corroboration is no longer a requirement for proof of rape in many states.

The word "rape" has been redefined, as laws are updated, to mean sexual battery or criminal sexual conduct. These and other broader legal definitions of rape are replacing the archaic language of common law. In Florida, it is interesting to note that men along with women are protected from "involuntary sexual battery."

While rape law reform is beginning to make progress, certainly the laws are in a state of flux. Because some states continue to have antiquated laws, many women who have been raped by strangers have lost cases because they did not exhibit enough resistance, even though they were threatened by a knife or gun.

Society's changing attitudes, and in turn, the passage of much rape law reform, is credited to the dedication and determination of women who have joined together in groups such as the National Organization for Women's Task Force on Rape. NOW's Task Force spans the nation through representatives in 200 chapters. These women work at both local and national levels to achieve their goals of obtaining just and humane treatment for rape victims, and major reforms and innovations as they relate to sex crimes. Their work in connection with a congressional bill to establish a National Center for the Prevention and Control of Rape is outstanding. The Task Force also works with the Congress in pressing for reforms and improved programs at national, state, and local levels.

What does this trend mean to the individual woman who has just been raped? Revised rape laws that are appearing in many states are slowly helping the innocent victims to obtain some justice even though they can never wipe out the tragedy. For example, in December of 1974, a man in New York State was convicted under the new rape law which abolished all requirements for corroboration of the victim's testimony. This made the testimony of a rape victim equal in weight to that of a person who had been robbed or mugged.

Long before a woman who has been raped reaches the question of deciding whether or not to take her case to court, she may report the crime to the police. Victims report a wide variation in the quality and type of care they have received from the police.

Consider the case of a young woman who has discussed what she would do if the need to cry rape ever became her personal problem. The young woman has been raped and left by the side of the road. She reaches a telephone and calls the hotline number 233–3000 which is familiar to her. She memorized it when she was attending a weekly consciousness-raising group in her apartment building. Here women had discussed the problem of rape, but the victim never really thought it would happen to her. Still the phone number was one that she remembers, and it is a comfort to know where to turn after being attacked by three men at gunpoint. The rape has taken place near New York City, and this rape reportline puts her in touch with the police unit that is trained to handle rape cases.

The rape victim who is familiar with a rape hotline, and the one who lives near a police department that is trained to handle rape cases, is both fortunate and unusual. Many women wonder whether or not they should even report to the police because they have heard of many cases where policemen have asked personal and insulting questions. A woman wonders if she might be able to identify the rapist, for during the rape she was thinking more about survival, pain, and personal problems than about the color of his eyes and other identifying characteristics. She saw him only at a time when she was frozen with terror. She wonders if her parents and neighbors will find out about the incident. No wonder many women question whether or not to call the police and report the rape. But for those who know a hotline number, the first step toward help is easy.

While the answers to a rape victim's questions vary in individual cases, there seems to be general agreement, nevertheless, that reporting a rape to the police helps in a number of ways. This does not mean that a person has to take the case to court. It does mean that each report will help to give the police a more accurate knowledge of the extent of the crime. If no one speaks up for the records, rape will not be considered the prevalent problem that it is. New statistics show a great increase in rape, and some of this is probably due to the fact that more women are reporting it.

What happens at a police station may be different for each person. Some women's experiences are very unpleasant, with policemen taking the attitude that the victim is the guilty one rather than the rapist. Many policemen do not understand the anxiety of a woman who has been recently raped. Some may treat the victim bruskly because they are embarrassed, while others treat them roughly because they do not believe that most are telling the truth. The police may consider most women to be the instigators of the sexual assault.

At such a time, a woman needs supportive care, and in some cities and towns, police are being trained to supply it. Many forces now have women on their staffs who are trained to handle rape cases. Most raped women appear to feel that only another woman can begin to understand their feelings of helplessness, anger, rage, and hysteria. In New York City, where the Sex Crimes Analysis Unit is a part of the city police department, a female detective interviews victims whenever possible.

The New York City Sex Crimes Analysis Unit is staffed by female investigators who have had previous experience in this type of work and are considered to be sensitive to the needs of women. The commanding officer is a police lieutenant, a woman who participates in various activities of the field operations. One of her activities is to inform people about her work. For example, she sometimes travels with a van that visits areas where there are large numbers of sexual attacks. The van, which is known as the Rape Coalition Outreach Van, draws a continual flow of visitors to see exhibits and talk with the women volunteers from various women's rights groups who ride in it. The volunteers are trained to educate others how to avoid and cope with rape. The exhibits instruct women on how to fend off an attacker and how one might prevent becoming a target for rape. It is mentioned that some rapists select the *place* for the rape in advance rather than the victim, and these potentially dangerous locations are pointed out. Volunteers in the van distribute copies of safety tips in English and in Spanish while various policewomen from the Sex Crimes Analysis Unit discuss prevention and self-defense with those who care to listen. Other women encourage people in the neighborhood to step inside the van.

Some boys as well as girls, and older women, visit the mobile information center in crime prone areas. For example, a boy who attended one demonstration insisted that he could protect himself because he could fight, but he seemed to want help in methods of self-defense. A police officer suggested that he read the pamphlet on self-defense and to stop hitchhiking. One mother, who visited the van with her two small children, came back later with her own mother. She felt that the children's grandmother could profit, too, by seeing some of the charts and talking with the women in the van. This mother remarked that she tells her girls to be careful but they respected the advice from the volunteers in the van more than her own.

In many parts of New York City, female detectives work with anti-rape groups and crisis intervention centers to help women who have just been raped. These groups also work together to develop public awareness of the rape problem and of the positive steps that can be taken to help prevent rape. They join together in speaking to community groups, colleges, and high school assemblies, and they try to enlist public support through the communication media and through their mutual cooperation.

Female police squads have a number of apparent advantages over males in rape task forces. Such women are sometimes more perceptive and sensitive to certain facts that are important and might have been overlooked by a male investigator during an interview. Many victims talk more freely with female police officers than they would with a male. But victims, on the other hand, have remarked that some women are callous while some men have a unique sensitivity which can be an asset in dealing with rape victims. For certain women, relating to an understanding man can help in readjustment, while for others, all men seem to be enemies. Whether or not all-female squads, or mixed squads are best is still a matter of debate.

Efforts are being made on many fronts and in many places to combat the problem of rape through training and improving procedures utilized by police departments, hospitals, and the criminal justice system. Unfortunately, relatively few women who are raped receive the kind of treatment that helps them most. However, it is rewarding to know that work is being done in this direction and that new efforts are being made in an increasingly greater number of places.

A team of researchers is presently studying ways of improving police investigation processes in New York. In Chicago, training bulletins have been issued concerning treatment of victims immediately after rape. They put emphasis on the fact that a police officer should be ever mindful that the victim is experiencing a shocking, embarrassing and terrifying ordeal and that the police role should be entirely supportive. The Chicago bulletin reminds police officers that during the acute state immediately following a sexual assault, the officer should serve as a model for reestablishing the victim's capacity to trust in others. The officer should also attempt to anticipate anxieties the victim may have as she copes with the rape experience. The tact and consideration extended to the victim during her initial contact with the police will probably play a large part in the outcome of a follow-up investigation. Certainly, it will help the victim to cope with the experience when emotional problems develop at a later time. Many find that police support can be open-minded without bias for or against the victim and can help both police and victim simultaneously.

In Washington, D.C., a task force has prepared a study through an exchange of ideas among members of the legal profession, the police department, the Commission on the Status of Women, the D.C. Rape Crisis Center, and the Women's Legal Defense Fund. This valuable report of the District of Columbia Task Force on Rape suggests, among other things, that one must ask "Why is rape treated differently from all other crimes and what are the results of this different treatment?" The report emphasizes that a central reason for the difference is the old feeling about women's sexuality. "A good woman is chaste," according to tradition. "Rape is a fate worse than death." If such is the case, a woman is expected to *fight* to avoid rape even if it means death. But it has been shown as fact that many women are frozen with fear and prevented from fighting if the rapist has a knife or a gun. According to police, they should not attempt to fight back at such a time.

Both in the District of Columbia Task Force study and in various police training bulletins, it is noted that there is a tendency to focus attention on whether or not the victim's complaint is bonafide, or on whether or not the woman is making false charges against a man—even a man she may not know. For many policemen, lack of physical injury may appear to mean lack of resistance, even though, paradoxically, women are told not to resist armed rapists. An uninformed or unsympathetic officer may be entirely unaware that a woman who has been raped is experiencing a deep emotional hurt, especially if there is no evidence of physical injury.

Many misunderstandings may arise during the woman's contact with the police. Handling rape victims is a common experience to the police in large cities, but for the victim it is very traumatic and unique. False accusations or threats of prosecution for lying may be made by police personnel, who tend to forget that the victim may never before have had to study a lineup, to look at photographs in a police station, or to face the problem of deciding whether or not she wants to appear before a grand jury if she prosecutes. The victim may not understand why various actions must be taken and may appear to be uncooperative. Hostility against the rapist may be expressed as hostility against all males at such a time.

One example of a police misunderstanding and an unfortunate attitude was dramatized at a recent seminar on rape at McGill University in Montreal, Canada. A woman gave a very moving description of what had happened to her when and after she was raped several years earlier. Her story made the audience of men and women empathize with her, for she was both sincere and distraught as she recalled the horrible experience which affected her dramatically through the next few years of her life. The need for understanding by those who are in contact with victims of rape was explored. The next speaker was a police officer who did not seem to have been moved by the rape victim's talk. He took the defensive approach and described several rape accusations brought to the attention of the police that were actually proved false as well as a true rape case. The women at the seminar reacted strongly against this man. If anyone was raped after hearing his point of view, it is unlikely that she would have been eager to call the police for help. This is just one instance of negative police response. Unfortunately, difficulties experienced by some policemen have made them intolerant of all rape victims.

Although it is true that the police must deal with some false accusations of rape, training and objective attitudes can help them distinguish, with greater efficiency, between false accusations and genuine cases. True rape victims seldom want public attention. Policemen who make false, hasty, or premature judgments are not only hurting the real victim emotionally, they are discouraging the reporting of a serious crime of violence.

The women who falsely accuse men of rape are sometimes those who are pressured by parents because of pregnancy. Some have other family problems. Many women who accuse falsely have any one of a variety of character disorders, and are of average or above average intelligence. Others are retarded and cannot appreciate the fact that the police department does not have time to help them punish their enemies or those who have slighted them. There are many case studies which bear witness to the fact that the motivations for false rape reports are numerous. Studies indicate that the percentage of rape complaints that are discovered to be unfounded is very low, and figures vary from less than 11 to 15 percent. Some false claims involve children. There are young girls who have claimed that their fathers or other members of their families have forcibly raped them. Examinations showed no evidence of this. Such girls have later admitted that they wanted more attention from their parents. Perhaps this was a way of attempting to get more attention, even though a desperate one. Some girls fantasize about rape and later admit that they reported what they wish had happened to them. School teachers and doctors are not infrequently the victims of false accusations by girls and women who have romantic attachments to them. Unwelcome stepfathers are sometimes victims of false rape accusations.

There are even reports of mothers who have claimed that their husbands raped their young daughters. This is a very difficult problem for all involved. For example, one pediatrician was asked to verify that a four-year-old girl had been raped. The mother publicly accused the father of the mistreatment. The father lost his position, he was ostracized by friends in the community and suffered in many other ways. After extensive psychiatric treatment, the mother confessed that she had falsely accused her husband, but this admission came too late for him to regain his losses. It did uncover a severe emotional illness in the mother.

Rape reports which reach police stations cover a very wide variety of situations, and police reaction varies even at the same police station. Each victim is different, each sexual assault is different, each rapist is different, and each police officer has a personal feeling about the rape. Some of the vibrations come through, both negative and positive, even after training.

Visualize a scene at a police station where the Sex Crimes Analysis Unit tries to help victims identify criminal suspects. Here, one might find several women who have been raped comparing their experiences and discussing how they feel at the moment. One is crying, another remarks casually that she has not been able to sleep for a week and has terrible nightmares. Another seems perfectly poised and explains that she has taken a course in karate, but could not use what she knew because of the weapon which was pointed at her.

Several detectives drive one of the women to the precinct in which she was attacked. There, at the Bureau of Criminal Identification, she looks through large numbers of mug shots. As she looks through them, she wonders if she might really be able to recognize any of the men. After a period of searching, she comes upon a picture of one possible suspect. She feels *almost* sure that this man was the one who had raped her, but she is not 100 percent sure. Then a detective who has a brisk, confident manner explains that her identification does not mean that the man will be imprisoned. He tells her that with the victim's information about this man's appearance, the police would search for him in the area in which the crime occurred. Her description of what the rapist was wearing, whether or not he had an accent, any identifying scars or moles, would help them. They would track down the activities of the man identified by the mug shot to substantiate whether he might have been in the area at the time of the crime.

Another approach to possible identification of the rapist is the use of a "Photo Fit" kit. This helps to produce a drawing of the attacker's face by means of familiar features that the victim identifies. For example, she looks through pages of different mouths until she comes to the one that she thinks is similar to the mouth of the rapist. She follows the same procedure with hairlines, noses, eyes, and chins. Then an artist puts these parts together in a special glass frame and the victim can change various features until the composite has some resemblance to the rapist.

If the police find a suspect who fits the description, the victim will be asked to identify him in person at a lineup or show-up. At that point, there may be an attorney for the suspect present to make sure that his rights are protected, as well as a police person who takes care of the victim. Women who have experienced rape find this a very unpleasant procedure even though they are assured that they cannot be seen through the glass which separates them from the suspect. The bright lights on the men who stand in front of a number on the wall make the men appear very different from the way they appeared when attacking the victim. The total environment is so different that many women are afraid that they will not choose the man who raped them. There have been occasional instances of false identification. Some women fear that a rapist will in some way hear and recognize their voices and search them out at some place to rape again.

While every effort should be made by police to encourage a woman to prosecute the rapist if there appears to be enough evidence, authorities agree that a woman should not be badgered into doing so. Information from all victims should be recorded to assist police investigations in the event similar patterns of rape recur in the future.

For the woman who decides to prosecute the rapist, the procedure may vary a great deal after she makes her statement at the police station and the hospital. What follows could depend on many things, including the circumstances of the rape, available evidence of rape, attitude of the defense attorney, and the ability of the rapist's attorney to confuse the victim. In some cases, plea bargaining takes place between the victim's state's attorney and the rapist's lawyer. This happens privately, and not in the presence of the victim. A "deal" is made in which the rapist pleads guilty to a charge less than rape and the case does not go to trial.

This means the victim does not have to go through the embarrassing details of the rape in open court. She may be willing to settle for such a situation, even though it means that the rapist is permitted to go free on parole, and is free to rape again.

If the case goes to trial, the woman and her lawyer must prove rape without a reasonable doubt. The trial may take place many months after the crime, and it may be a long and very unpleasant procedure. As mentioned earlier, the verdict of guilty is not often reached. Conviction rates are very, very low indeed. In fact, of the rapists arrested and charged, only about 10 percent are actually convicted of rape.

Many women are joining with men doing research on the justice system in its efforts to make rape sentencing lighter. Penalties for rape are so severe in many states that juries tend not to bring in a verdict of guilty, especially if the rapist's attorney has been clever in his handling of the case.

New court procedures for rape cases are rapidly being introduced. In some places, for example, the woman has the right to ask that the courtroom be cleared, and if the judge feels it is necessary, he or she will do so.

In Philadelphia there is a new phone call system which helps victims avoid hours of waiting in court on the day they receive their subpoenas. The District Attorney's office will phone the woman about an hour before her case is called, or at whatever time they feel necessary, to give the woman enough time to get to the courtroom comfortably.

Many innovations in procedure are the result of work by women's groups such as local rape crisis centers, NOW Task Force on Rape chapters, and other groups which are forcing change by social and political pressure.

Change is based partly on new knowledge gained by research. If new laws result in more prosecutions, they may serve to remove dangerous persons from society and act as a deterrent to some degree. But feminists feel that convicted rapists will repeat their acts of rape and the roots of the problem lie in the sexism of society. A rapist may feel that women are powerful and dominant and that only by rape can he humiliate a female and obtain revenge. This helps him to feel more powerful than the female he forces into submission. In such a case, the motivation is considered only remotely sexual. If the whole basis of action is the Strong Male vs. the Weak Female, rape will continue no matter how laws are changed. If a male no longer needs to feel powerful and dominant, or any of the other long-touted masculine qualities, will he need to rape?

Much research remains to be done, but the amount is increasing and greater numbers of men and women *are* changing their attitudes toward rape. Many agencies which deal with the legal aspects of rape are now reviewing procedures and recognizing that in the past, rape received widespread, inadequate treatment. Many innovations are being designed to remedy past defects in the system, but the changes are too limited in number so far to help many recent victims.

Guidelines for rape law reform are still being researched by some states which have not already made changes. If anyone is interested in what is considered especially good by large numbers of people, including Mary Ann Largen, Coordinator of NOW's National Task Force on Rape, Michigan's new laws are a good example. This state has taken a bold, progressive step by revising its century-old rape statute. With the combined efforts of the governor, the legislature and interested women's groups, Michigan has a "model" law that has received national acclaim.*

The new law, Public Act 266 of 1974, includes these key points:

> There are four degrees of criminal sexual conduct with appropriate penalties. In the past, many law enforcement authorities ignored sexual assault cases when the victim was not seriously injured. Now there is a specific crime for different factual circumstances, making prosecution easier.
>
> Evidence of the victim's past sexual activity is not admissible, unless it involves the accused, or may prove the origin of disease or pregnancy. Even with these two specific exceptions, the trial judge must

*Michigan's complete laws are given on pages 119 to 129.

hold a private hearing in his chambers to determine if the value of the evidence as a test outweighs its inflammatory nature.

"Resistance to the utmost" by the victim is no longer required. Thus, victims faced with an assault by a weapon need not resist if it would be futile or dangerous to do so.

Persons who have filed for divorce or separation and are living apart are protected from sexual assault by their spouses.

Both male and female victims are protected by the new law.

Corroboration of the victim's testimony is not required; meaning evidence of the assault, such as injuries or torn clothing, is not necessary.

You can find out what your own community is doing about rape reform laws by contacting human rights departments in your local area or state capital, women's crisis centers, feminist groups, your local representative to the state senate, your local prosecuting attorney, or any group interested in the rights and status of women.

Letters from women who support changes in the rape laws of a state help to get action. If you find that the laws in your state are archaic or would do little to help you or a friend who might be raped, now is the time to act.

In Search of Knowledge About Rape

Research on the subject of rape brings to light controversial viewpoints. What one thinks about the subject depends, in part, on the sex of the person who is doing the thinking. Each individual is programmed to some degree by early training and attitudes about sex. This affects ability to identify with the rapist or with the victim of rape. Even various feminist groups disagree about the role of women in society and about their feelings in their relationships with men. Viewpoints vary widely. On one end of the scale are the radical feminists who maintain that the rapist is any man— even a friend, husband or apparently normal neighbor and that rape is the logical expression of the present essential relationship between men and women. Only changing attitudes about sex will help to prevent the number of rapes from growing. On the opposite end of the scale from the radical feminists are those women who accept their fate as inferior to males. They say: "Woman's most satisfying role is that of satisfying her husband's needs."

Before the work of Menachem Amir was published in 1971, few men or women contributed anything toward the research literature that has since helped to change public attitudes. Amir's study was based on an intensive evaluation and interpretation of rape cases in the Philadelphia Police Department files. Although he covered only a period of the years 1958 and 1960, these were seen as representative years for valid analysis, and his studies were supported with more than 500 reference sources. It has already become a very important book for anyone researching the problems of rape, and has taken its place as one of the first important studies.

Since the time of the appearance of Amir's *Patterns in Forcible Rape,* both male and female researchers have begun to explore the subject in far larger numbers than ever before. One researcher who does not agree with the "old-fashioned" attitude that "women invite rape" does believe that many rapes occur because women place themselves at undue risk. Another male researcher who is exploring the rape problem states that prevention mainly rests with the woman, who must not expose herself unnecessarily to danger. Feminists agree that women can help to protect themselves from rape through various means, such as avoiding walking alone at night, but they argue that women should not be so restricted.

Understanding of why rape occurs is far from complete. Most research on the subject that is meaningful in today's world is extremely recent, and only a very few of the new projects are mentioned in the following pages. It may be noted that some of the subjects being explored overlap. This is not entirely bad, for comparisons can be made when conclusions have been drawn.

An investigation which played a part in legislative changes was the Prince George's County Task Force project to study the treatment of the victims of sexual assault in Prince George's County, Maryland. Some of the conclusions highlighted by the report were:

> While a woman has been brought up to be passive, she is expected to fight the rapist.

> A woman is treated as an object, a piece of evidence, and is made to relive her rape experience when questioned at the police station, the hospital, and in court.

> Serious psychological stress after rape may be largely due to the guilt and shame imposed by society. A woman may not recognize her need for professional help or may not be able to afford it at a time when she needs it. This time may be long after the assault.

> The effect of rape on the psyche of a woman cannot be accurately measured. Some women recover; some do not. But there is no question as to whether or not the entire family of the victim is affected, for they are.

> It is recommended that there is a complete overhauling of procedures used in dealing with rape victims, from

immediately after the rape through the years that follow.

The report by the Task Force of Prince George's County and the one undertaken by the District of Columbia, mentioned on page 55, make substantial contributions to a better understanding of the dimensions of the problem of rape. Their work along with that of others, influenced efforts toward a National Center for Control and Prevention of Rape. These studies point out that the system for responding to rape in many communities is not only defective, but also harmful to the victim. They hope to reveal the impact of rape on the victim's family and the community, and assist members of a community to understand the sense of fear, rejection, and even anger which is experienced by women because their lives are shaped by the persistent threat of rape. This calls for a continued search for the truth about rape, its personal consequences, and its social implications.

One particularly interesting research study now in progress deals with the *possibility* of a causal relationship between alcohol and rape. It is under the direction of Dr. Richard T. Rada, Assistant Professor of Psychiatry and Associate Director of Research at the University of New Mexico School of Medicine in Albuquerque.

Dr. Rada emphasizes that the casual association between alcoholism and rape does not necessarily imply a cause-and-effect relationship. Since the rapists who have been studied are those who have been caught, it is possible that the sample studied is not fairly balanced or truly representative of all rapists, but it is nevertheless one of the limited number of research studies on rapists.

Along with others, Dr. Rada believes that rape is not only the fastest-growing reported crime of violence in the United States, but that the increase is real—not one simply due to increased reporting. He also notes that alcoholism is the number one drug abuse problem, and there is a widely held belief that alcohol is associated with violent sexual offenses. Research has exploded the myth of the "typical alcoholic." This person is no longer thought of as an ineffectual, passive-aggressive personality. Scientists now generally accept the fact that there are a large variety of personality types as well as drinking patterns among alcoholics. Dr. Rada remarks in an article titled "Alcohol and Rape" in *Medical Aspects of Human Sexuality* that there is neither a typical alcoholic nor a typical rapist. On the other hand, there does seem to be a significant association between forcible rape and the presence of alcohol. This does not mean that most rapists are alcoholics nor that alcohol intake or alcoholism in itself leads to rape behavior. However, it is interesting to note, that according to Dr. Sidney Cohen of U.C.L.A., half the rapes occur while the aggressor is under the influence of alcohol. Perhaps the less cunning rapists, or those more disturbed, are most likely to get caught.

For the nonalcoholic rapist, Dr. Rada suggests that

drinking prior to the rape acts as a psychic muscle-builder, allowing him to overcome his timidity with members of the female sex. The pattern of using alcohol to bolster self-esteem has frequently been found in the case of married men who are having sexual difficulty with their wives.

Little attention has been paid to the relationship between drinking and forcible rape and even less to the relationship between alcoholism and rape. Dr. Rada reports the following information. In a recent study of 77 rapists who were committed to the Atascadero State Hospital in California, 50 percent of the rapists were drinking at the time of the offense, and the alcoholism rate was established at 35 percent. In another of his studies, he dealt with 122 rapists who had been committed to prison at Atascadero State Hospital. Of these, 57 percent admitted drinking at the time of the offense.

While much remains to be learned about the alcoholic rapist, the act of rape appears to be just one more type of behavior in his series of maladaptive and self-destructive behaviors. In Dr. Rada's research, the speculation that alcohol acts as a specific chemical trigger in certain males is being explored. For some people, it appears that different sexual fantasies, desires and sensations are aroused when they are under the influence of alcohol than when they are not.

There are a number of theories about the relationship between alcohol and rape. One suggests that alcohol impairs judgment, and reduces inhibitions toward socially unacceptable actions. Dr. Rada agrees with this theory for most people but he does not believe that the drinking of alcoholic beverages necessarily takes away the sexual inhibitions of the rapist. Dr. Rada leans toward the hypothesis of authorities who feel that men drink to feel stronger rather than to reduce anxiety. Here again is an illustration of the desire for control and power, rather than a desire for some kind of sexual fulfillment. According to Dr. Rada's report, a fact that stands out is the relatively nonsexual aspect of the act of rape. The rapists seemed to focus on their aggressive and assertive behavior when they were interviewed, for this seemed to be the area about which they were most concerned. Alcohol appears to be the perfect drug for the rapist, in the sense that it may act as a stimulus to increase his sense of power and willingness to engage in a sexual act that he would ordinarily find himself unable to attempt.

Dr. Rada does not suggest that his studies are sufficient to indicate a causal relationship between alcohol and rape, but he feels that this possibility warrants more investigation, since those who treat sex offenders should look for signs of proneness toward addiction. If a drinking or alcoholic rapist can bring his drinking under control, he may no longer be a rapist. This is an area for further research.

An entirely different type of research is being carried out by Dr. Shirley Feldman-Summers, an Assistant Professor in the Department of Psychology at the University of Washington in Seattle. Dr. Feldman-Summers is focusing upon the question of whether rape victims report assaults, and whether they utilize social services designed for them. This research project is being supported by a grant from the National Institute of Mental Health and is one which may add considerably to our knowledge about many aspects of rape. In other research projects she is also exploring characteristics of the victims, the alleged assailants, and the circumstances surrounding the assault, which may influence judgments and decisions made about the rape by police, prosecutors, members of juries, and other people associated with the criminal justice system. More about her work is described in the last chapter of this book.

One of the major researchers in the area of forcible rape is Duncan Chappell of Batelle Memorial Institute in Seattle, Washington. In 1973, he co-authored a study with Susan Singer, in which material on rape in the police files of New York City was analyzed and compared with earlier studies, including that of Mena-chim Amir. The authors drew the conclusion that the vast majority of rape charges were dismissed on the basis of lack of corroboration of the victim's story. It was through this additional proof requirement that rape was clearly singled out from other crimes for special treatment. Since many states, including New York, have now dropped this requirement, there is hope that more rapists will be removed from the streets, and that more convictions will encourage more reporting and other positive steps.

One of the conclusions which this report found particularly disturbing was the excessive number of data deficiencies relating to forcible rape in the New York City police files prior to 1973. The missing facts, in many cases, comprised the evidence that seemed crucial for the successful handling of the cases by the prosecution and the courts. The same study observed that the way the victim is treated by the police is an important element. However, with a new rape squad in action in New York City and with a new approach adopted by the entire system, a new era of criminal justice may have begun.

Dr. Duncan Chappell presented a report at the Symposium on Justice and the Behavioral Sciences, "Rape-Research Action Prevention," which was held in 1975 at the University of Alabama. Here he told of a study being made to survey present practices in the criminal justice system relating to forcible rape. Comprehensive questionnaires have been sent out to a random sample of 200 police agencies and prosecutors' offices throughout the U.S. with the intent of providing baseline data on existing criminal justice procedures concerning this crime. The content of the questionnaires covers problems associated with the investigation, apprehension and prosecution of offenders. He is attempting to obtain information about personnel and training needs, and to discover new and innovative programs and procedures within agencies. He has included questions about suggestions for reforms that are thought to be desirable.

This research project is being carried out over a period of two years. In addition to the questionnaires the project will include in depth examinations of innovative rape programs adopted by criminal justice agencies in at least five locations around the United States. One of these programs is already being studied in Seattle.

Part of Dr. Chappell's research effort includes interviews with 100 victims of forcible rape. In addition to the victim interviews, about 50 rapists have been interviewed from a sample of 300. The central objective of this portion of the research project is to describe and analyze forcible rape patterns. A detailed knowledge of the specific mode of action, or *modus operandi,* of rapists should help in the education of potential victims and the apprehension of offenders. Material such as previous sex offense records, choice of victim, interaction, weapons, post-rape interaction, and advice to women have been examined. The subjects were permitted to remain anonymous and each interview was tape-recorded to assure complete coverage.

A future aspect of the research project in which Dr. Chappell is involved is a comprehensive assessment of current legislative and allied developments related to forcible rape. This survey can be a valuable resource for those wishing to keep up with the rapidly changing rape laws. Model guidelines for handling forcible rape cases by the police and prosecutors, as well as guide-lines for the prevention of forcible rape and for victim treatment and counseling, are being developed by Dr. Chappell and his associates in the midst of a constantly changing scene.

Still another area of research is in the recording and reporting of forcible rape cases. Dr. Chappell and colleagues in an earlier study revealed that there has been a lack of comparative research in this area in the past. The 40,000 or more police forces in the United States use a variety of systems in recording cases of rape. Comparing police records in two cities, Boston and Los Angeles, it is obvious that there is much variation in reporting due to differences in the defini-tion of rape. In Los Angeles virtually any instance in which a rapist seems to be seeking "sexual gratifica-tion" was apt to be classified as forcible rape. In Boston the rate of rape appeared to be low until the fact was discovered that victims had to "suffer a fate worse than death" to become a forcible rape statistic. Statutory rape, in which no force is employed and the victim is under legal age, as well as other variations of forcible rape, were eliminated by the Boston definition.

Researchers in the field of rape are among the first to admit that the problem of rape prevention has been relatively neglected by law enforcement agencies, behavioral scientists, and by the medical and legal professions. Dr. James L. Burkes of the Chicago Lying-In Hospital suggests the following four areas where help and progress in the field of rape might be possible. They seem similar to some of the goals of grass-roots crisis centers which women are forming:

1. Education of the population on the problem of rape and what the individual can do for self-protection.
2. Increased police protection.
3. A system of humane treatment, support, and follow-up once the event has occurred.
4. A change in the legal system which now puts the victim on the defensive and almost requires that she subject herself to physical harm to verify the event.

Some states, as mentioned earlier, have already changed laws in this direction. These suggestions were made at a symposium on rape which was reported by the Journal of Reproductive Medicine in April of 1974.

At this symposium, the participants explored many areas and concluded along with many other men who are fighting rape that confrontation and lack of credibility seem to be the "name of the game." Because of this the rape victim often encounters hostility rather than understanding and support in a caring environment which is extremely important for her future. Here again, one finds experts saying the same thing as women who have explored the situation with less professional help.

The Chaplaincy Services Department of the University of Chicago under the direction of the Reverend H. Rex Lewis has been providing supportive care to rape victims who have been brought to the Adult Emergency Rooms of the University of Chicago Hospitals and clinics since March of 1972. Here, some of the goals mentioned above are already in action.

As early as March, 1973, Dr. Lewis presented a workshop paper at the annual meeting of the College of Chaplains where the members of the American Protestant Hospital Association were joining in an effort to approve counseling programs for rape victims. He described how a counseling program for rape victims was developed using a staff of various professional and service people at the University of Chicago. Services are provided to all alleged rape victims under a system designated "Code R."* The procedures for Code R are as follows:

The University of Chicago Hospitals and Clinics "CODE R" Procedures for Chaplains

1. *Triage Officer* **Screens patient; if the patient is in physical trauma she will be directed to the examining area immediately. If patient's physical needs are not deemed "urgent" she will be referred to the clerk for necessary registration information and then referred by clerk to Chaplain's conference room if she is not alone.**

2. *Triage Officer* **Pages Chaplain for "Code R" in Billings Emergency. (After midnight the clerk will page the Chaplain.)**

*Reprinted with permission from the University of Chicago Hospitals and Clinics.

3. *Chaplain*   Responds to conference room and/or triage officer (E.R. extension is 7-5411).

4. *Chaplain*   Coordinates situation:
   a. Accompanies patient to conference room if she is not already there.
   b. Provides support, not counseling (context of grief work).
   c. Assesses needs (focus of concern):
      (1) Patient's own needs for support.
      (2) Assures patient that arrangements for medical exam are being made. (Clerk is instructed to phone conference room when examining room is ready for patient. Chaplain may find it helpful to ask clerk for estimate of waiting period.)
      (3) Family notification. (Chaplain assesses who has been contacted and who might be contacted and when.)
   d. When possible, prepares patient and is present for police involvement. (Note: 1] By law, police must be called. 2] Frequently police bring rape victims to the hospital.)

5. If the Chaplain is paged for another emergency he will assess priority and decide if another Chaplain is to be called in to cover this second emergency.

6. In general, Chaplain will facilitate supportive care and discharge of patient as soon as possible. Chaplain will make sure that transportation arrangements have been made.

7. Chaplain will offer follow-up care arrangements, suggesting that patient return to speak with a Chaplain (sheet to be provided).

Rape victims appear to welcome the supportive and nonthreatening role provided by the men associated with religion. Chaplains and the staff function as a team. Since the emotional needs of the victims are handled by the chaplains, busy doctors who are frequently fatigued and frustrated are relieved of this responsibility.

One form of counseling which is offered by the chaplaincy program, as well as by a number of others, recognizes the victim's need for psychological support even when she *denies* that need. She may want to avoid the public attention that may be associated with follow-up care or she may be going through a pseudo adjustment period. At such a time, the victim appears to have resolved all her problems.

As many as 85 to 90 percent of the victims studied in this program responded to the experience of rape with acute anxiety. After the feelings of confusion, fear, and a sense of being very ashamed subside, other fears appear. Many victims feel that they are rejected by family and friends, and in some cases they are. The rape experience may pose a problem with a male associate, whether the victim is married or not.

In the program, a counselor is trained to respond to and recognize fears of a rape victim and to help her explore plans for handling such matters. Just the ability to express fear and explore imagined reactions from those people with whom she is closely involved may help her to mobilize strength. Providing supportive care includes assistance in re-establishing the victim's capacity to experience trust in other people. A healing process must take place to enable the victim to learn to trust in the presence of hurt and fear.

Research shows that rape is a socially unacceptable trauma and this makes it particularly difficult for the victim. Mugging or appendicitis or a death in the family evoke support and concern of friends. Rape seldom does.

Chaplain Lewis reports in his studies of rape victims that they typically react to their experience by undergoing several changes that affect their life-style. Along with anxiety, and the feeling of being dirtied and shamed, victims frequently express feelings of guilt that are real or imagined about their part in the rape. They need emotional support and an opportunity to share these feelings, and to affirm, for themselves, their lack of complicity in the rape. Other deep-seated emotional difficulties seem to surface at a crisis time and changes in geographical location and occupation are frequent. Here, as in so many other studies, it is noted that the whole life pattern of the victim may be altered due to rape.

On his research for both the symposiums mentioned earlier and the report presented at an American Protestant Hospital Association meeting, Dr. Lewis reports, "Many of the victims of rape seemed to have no logical, rational way of preventing the rape. They were individuals who were picked up beside the bus stop, or whose car was forced to a stop on the way to work, or whose home was broken into on a forced-entry/robbery/rape experience. Their only logical choice for the avoidance of rape is to become a recluse, and even that is no guarantee.

"Other rape victims had broken the basic principles of protection and suspicion needed to survive in certain urban areas. They were guilty of security slips—a door was left open in the home or apartment, or the victim took an evening walk alone or without a dog. Many of these victims said, in effect, 'I knew better than to have taken the chance, but I thought, just this one time.'

"Others, for whatever reasons, conscious or unconscious, found themselves in situations or relationships which tended to invite the possibility of rape. While I personally endorse equal rights for women, including the right to enter a bar unescorted late in the night, many of the victims we have seen are testimony that some in society view this action as an invitation to sexual involvement or rape."*

One area in which research is already bearing fruit is the study of victimology. Many authorities agree that a definite pattern follows the experience of rape in almost all victims. The symptoms of the first few days show the victim appearing to be anxious, dismayed, shocked, distressed, angry, and experiencing some of the other feelings mentioned earlier. Then a few weeks pass while the victim appears to be adjusted and to have accepted the facts as they are. It is in this

*Quoted with permission.

period of pseudo adjustment that Chaplain Lewis has found help to be lacking. After a number of weeks, the rape victim enters a third stage in which she may well be depressed and unable to cope with things in general. Some victims suffer from nightmares, are unable to carry on jobs, and get little or no pleasure or satisfaction from life experiences which once were enjoyed. Victims may have trouble relating to others and some suffer from sexual difficulties so severe that they lead to divorce or suicide. The impact of rape on the life of the victim varies, but in the overwhelming majority of cases, it has a very damaging effect.

In order to learn more about the effects of rape on a victim's personality, Dr. Joseph J. Peters is making an excellent study in Philadelphia where he is Director of the Center for Rape Concern at the Philadelphia General Hospital (P.G.H.) and Senior Staff Psychiatrist at the Institute of Pennsylvania Hospital. Since former studies were limited in number and scope, and since police reports offer statistics which tend to view rape victims as a group rather than as individuals, Dr. Peters and his colleagues (six psychiatrists, six social workers and research personnel) developed a program which attempts to provide personal help for the victim based on extensive social and psychological data being collected. Although the aim was much the same as the chaplaincy program described earlier, many aspects differ.

Dr. Peters' studies emphasize that the emotional climate surrounding rape can be so intense that the *responses* of the victim, her family, and the community can be both irrational and insensitive. Even though a community and its service organizations will react with initial shock at rape and intense concern for the victim, the authorities' interest in the victim is soon ended if the offender is not apprehended for trial. The P.G.H. Center for Rape Concern was established in the fall of 1970 to focus on the problems of rape victims. Its objectives are: first, to study the social and psychological effects of rape upon females, and correlate the different victim reactions with pre-rape personality; to study circumstances surrounding the rape and support mechanisms of "significant others," including community reaction and rehabilitative services. Second, to study the effects of the criminal justice system on the victim.

In this Philadelphia program, female social workers conduct extensive home-interviews with alleged victims of rape within forty-eight hours after treatment at the P.G.H. emergency room, where they are customarily brought by the police. Psychiatric evaluation is made available soon after the home visitor makes her call. Psychiatric evaluations have been conducted at home when necessary. The victim may reject the psychiatric help, but the home visitor calls every three or four months for a year. If she finds that the rape crisis has precipitated extensive problems which frequently involve the victim's family, referral to community mental health services is made, or other recommendations for help arranged. Center for Rape Concern psychiatrists continue with those victims whose symptoms seem primarily related to the rape incident.

This program seems to succeed in helping victims where others fail, due, at least in part, to the fact that help is made available through home visits both immediately after the assault and at a later time when post-rape reactions frequently go unrecognized.

Protection
and Prevention

Actually, very little is known about how a woman should act when attacked by a rapist. Some of the research which is being done has been described earlier in this book. All researchers, no matter whether they are professional people or women who are spearheading the movement to improve help for rape victims, want to remedy the horrible abuse often suffered by such victims. Feminists want to help, and there are many groups of women organized against rape. Some women feel that the fight against rape should be a fight carried on entirely by women. Groups such as NOW invite men to join them. A recently organized group, MOAR, is Men Organized Against Rape. Many of the men who join such groups have been indirectly affected by rape because they are related in some way to women who have suffered assault and feel strongly about changing the present laws and treatment of rape victims.

Instructions on how to act if attacked by a rapist are plentiful, but they are contradictory in some cases. Should one fight back? Should one faint, struggle, scream? Should one run away? Since each rape has different circumstances, there is no general answer to this question. Each rapist is different from all others. Each person who is attacked, whether male or female, is different from all others. And the environment in which the rape takes place is never exactly the same. In spite of this, knowing the techniques of dealing with sexual assault may help you to survive physically and to suffer less traumatic aftereffects. Such knowledge might protect you from rape, and possibly physical injury.

If you are a woman consider what you would do in the following circumstances. If you are a man what would you advise a woman to do? Suppose you are studying in a cubicle at the library late in the afternoon when the building is deserted. A young man appears nearby and asks for directions to another part of the campus. You are not aware of any danger until he pushes you into a nearby room and demands that you remove your clothing. You keep telling yourself this isn't really happening but you become very tense. The need for self-protection is your most important feeling, so you comply with his wishes. At the same time, you try to reason with the man by asking him if he would treat his sister this way. You try to persuade the young man that he should not rape you, but at this point, he pulls out a knife and threatens to stab your throat. From then on, you do not look at him or attempt to resist.

In this case, the woman to whom this actually happened was stabbed in the chest and severely injured. She was so preoccupied with the fear and the humility of the sexual assault that she did not realize until later how severely she had been cut. Actually, open heart surgery was necessary to save her life. Later, as her body was mending, she began to think again and again of what she might have done to prevent the rape. She wondered what she could have done to prevent the physical damage. She kept going over the experience in her mind, questioning her own actions, even though she was the victim of the assault.

Even after this young woman left the hospital, she thought again and again of the incident in the library. She pretended that she had been able to overcome the man physically. At other times, she fantasized that someone had come to the room and rescued her from the situation. Through psychiatric support, she was helped to cope with her physical and emotional problems. The healing process took a long time.

One of the things which aided the situation was the fact that the victim of the rape had participated in consciousness-raising groups, rape crisis center meetings, and educational workshops which dealt with such emergencies. She had not closed her eyes to the fact that the situation of rape is one that is real, although, typically, she never thought it would happen to her.

Is there anything which this woman could have done to prevent what happened to her? Many people would suggest that she should not have been studying in a room in a deserted part of the building. Many women would respond that she had a right to be there. Researchers would say no one really knows how this person could have handled the situation better, for the rapist had a knife and was ready to use it. According to some advice, she might have found a time in which she could have escaped if she had initially pretended to go along with the rape and had not antagonized the man by trying to reason with him. On the other hand, some say this might have been an invitation to murder. This girl expressed her fear but the rapist continued in spite of it.

There have been cases on record where a rapist will empathize with a frightened woman. Consider the case of Mary, who is a fifteen-year-old girl. One afternoon Mary decided to walk home from school along the railroad tracks rather than take her usual route. The leaves were changing color. Mary just felt like being alone to enjoy the colors and the silence of the woods and think private thoughts. Good feelings welled up inside her, until suddenly a man grabbed her from behind. Mary started to scream but the man held one hand over her mouth. Her good feelings had changed to fright. But she stopped screaming, regained her cool, and told the man how frightened she was at his sudden appearance. Mary apologized to the stranger for screaming and tried to get him to talk about his problems.

In this case the recognition of the woman's fear and her empathy were enough to satisfy the rapist, whose main desire, in this case, was for power over a woman. He examined his own feelings and began to wonder why he was attempting to rape this young girl. Mary's confidence in herself and ability to use techniques to bring her attacker under control saved her. Although in any kind of crisis such as this, one's ability to make decisions and think clearly are impaired, thinking ahead about what one would do in case of an emergency helps. Unfortunately, this does not mean that all rapists will react the way this man did. Some will not be deterred no matter what actions a woman takes.

Many women advise screaming "Fire!" if one is attacked. Some men have a tendency to become hostile at any sign of resistance while others back away from the scene when the victim resists. A woman who is being attacked has no way of knowing how a rapist will react. Each must assess the individual case as best she can, remembering that survival is more important than anything else at such a time.

Recently in New York City a man entered a third floor apartment through the rear window and attempted to rape a woman at three o'clock in the morning in her own bedroom. In this case the victim's roommate was a policewoman trained in the use of a weapon. The man who was threatening rape began to undress, but as he did, the potential victim screamed to her roommate who appeared on the scene. She was threatened with a large kitchen knife, but after wrestling with him, the roommate managed to reach her service revolver. When the man came at her again, she told him she was a police officer and fired a shot at his leg. He shouted "I'm going to cut your throat!" but he was in no condition to do so. He was taken to Bellevue Hospital where the bullet wound was treated. The man was booked on charges of attempted murder, burglary, attempted rape, and possession of a dangerous weapon.

Many women who read about this case wonder if through plea bargaining the rape charge will be dropped when this case comes to trial, and whether it will go on the record as a burglary attempt.

The use of a revolver in the above case was a good one, but few women room with police officers. The question of whether or not a woman should possess a legal weapon to protect herself against rape is extremely controversial. Most authorities feel that instead of its being used in self-defense, the rapist may wrest it from her and use it against her. In many cases, such a weapon may not be nearby when a woman is attacked. For certain women, attempts to resist may increase her fear reaction without providing real protection. For others, it may be a means of staying calm. Some of this difference will depend on a woman's training in defense tactics and in her ability to handle a weapon.

When a gun is used after rape, it may involve complications for a woman. One celebrated case in California is that of Inez Garcia who was found guilty of murder after she killed the companion of a man who allegedly raped her. In this case, the gun was in revenge rather than self-defense. Joan Little's case is another famous one. She was accused of murder after killing a jailer who allegedly attempted to rape her in her cell. She claimed she stabbed him in self-defense. There was much evidence to substantiate her claims and many people throughout the United States sent financial support for her trial and she was acquitted. But the fact remains that in using a weapon against a potential rapist, it can be difficult to prove self-defense.

For those women who feel strongly against the use of weapons such as guns and knives, the following methods of self-defense are frequently recommended. Do you think they are practical?

> A plastic lemon will squirt quite far. When filled with a liquid such as ammonia, it may be possible to reach the eyes of the rapist, momentarily blinding him so that the victim has time to get away.
> Hair sprays, perfume, and similar materials may serve the same purpose as a plastic lemon when used in similar manner.
> A large hatpin carried in the hand may be used to jab near the neck or scrape across the face.

An umbrella may be used for a quick jab to the neck, stomach, or face.

A key held between the fingers can injure the man's face and allow time for your escape.

You can smash the attacker's nose with your head or use an upward blow with the palm of your hand.

The side of the hand can be used to chop at the attacker's Adam's apple.

You can aim at his eyes with two fingers to injure him and distract him long enough to escape.

Kicking in the groin has been a much publicized method of defense, but it is extremely difficult for a woman to injure a rapist this way unless she is extremely strong, and the rapist happens to be in a vulnerable position.

Scratching the face with fingernails and using the teeth, if the rapist is close enough, are suggested by some as a means of defense.

A lighted cigarette smashed into the area of the face may be one of the better methods of attack.

Some women have been successful in protecting themselves by clapping both hands over the man's ears or pulling his hair so that he is distracted long enough for them to escape.

Remember that much depends on whether or not you can catch the attacker off guard. If he anticipates your throwing your hands out to strike him, he can grab you.

There are those who disagree with the attempt to defend oneself from a rapist by these methods. They point out, for example, that although the Adam's apple is a vulnerable spot on the man's body, most men will not be incapacitated by a blow to this area. Other methods of attack such as jabbing with a pen, key, or hatpin, etc. are good only if one uses them at the proper moment to distract the rapist, and can escape. Even if one studies karate or judo, it's quite possible that the rapist has a weapon and your attack may provoke him to use that weapon. No matter what kind of self-defense a woman attempts, it is possible that the rapist can overwhelm her either physically or by the use of weapons. He may even have a friend or friends hidden nearby who will come to his aid if he is attacked.

A woman who has provoked a rapist may create additional hostility in an already aggravated man. On the other hand, she may scare him away. Knowledge of these possiblities does not provide much help to a potential victim. The answers to this problem are far from clear. One beginning step in the right direction is *awareness* of the *problem* of rape, a major purpose of this book. Actions of many kinds are needed, especially in encouraging research and education.

The following rather famous rape case has led to some positive action. A young woman was walking from one building on campus to another at about eleven o'clock at night at the university which she attended in the Washington, D.C. area. She was attacked by a man, dragged into a nearby building and viciously raped. The guard on campus walked by, and, although he heard the noises of the woman attempting to call for help, he did not investigate. While the woman tried to protect herself from the rapist, she was aware that the most important thing was to survive. She cooperated with him and went through with the rape, realizing that this was less harmful than being knifed or killed. Although it is true that comparatively few rapists do murder, one never knows which ones will, and this particular man held a knife at her throat. While she used her head and tried to retain her composure, she suffered considerably from the experience both at the time, and for many years afterward.

The case was brought to trial, an experience that was almost as bad as the rape. In this case, the man was freed even though he confessed, because of a legal technicality. Today this young woman is making efforts to help in the formation of feminist groups to fight rape. Although she has moved to a different city and has gradually learned to talk freely about her experience, it has left its scar. The positive outcome of her tragic experience is the part it played in the formation of one of the most active women's crisis centers in the country. Since that time many other rape crisis centers have gone into action and are continuing to add to the pressures of the fight by women against rape.

Until the fight against rape is at least partly won, many women protect themselves by avoiding certain situations. Certainly, a woman has as much right to walk in dark areas as a man, but her chances of being raped are far greater than those of a man who might (but who probably would not), in a similar situation, be attacked and overcome by another man. In the rape-prevention tactics that have been compiled by many groups of people, it is often suggested that women avoid dark areas that are not populated.

Suggestions for avoiding rape on the street include walking at a steady pace and appearing confident. This apparently does make a great difference in whether or not a rapist picks out a woman for attack. Many authorities consider confidence a more important deterrent than type of clothing. Shoes that are a hindrance in running should be avoided. A woman is advised to cross a street rather than walk through a group of men. She should walk at the curb side of a sidewalk rather than close to buildings and avoid bushes, alley entrances, and driveways. If possible, one should avoid hitchhiking, since this is dangerous for women travelling alone or even in pairs. Group rapists and single rapists are known to cruise about looking for women hitchhikers whom they can transport to a place for attack without interference. As suggested earlier, if one must hitchhike, a woman driver is probably safer than a man. Further suggestions for those who hitchhike may be obtained from many women's crisis centers.

TEACHING CHILDREN TO PROTECT THEMSELVES FROM THE CHILD MOLESTER*

The Rape Task Force of the National Organization for Women suggests the following ways to teach children to protect themselves from child molesters:

*Reprinted with permission of NOW Task Force on Rape.

1. It is very important that children be taught *caution,* not fear.
2. Children should likewise be taught a new definition of "stranger":

   A stranger is somebody you have never seen before or *somebody you don't know as well as you think you might.*

Parents and teachers can use a representative list of acquaintances, semiacquaintances and would-be acquaintances to help the child understand the "stranger" concept.

3. The following rules, provided by the Akron, Ohio, Police Department can serve as an excellent checklist for parental and teacher guidance:

   - Never accept a ride in a car from a stranger or from someone you don't know very well. Sometimes these people will have plausible excuses. They may ask, "Will you show me where the Wilsons live? I can't seem to find their house," or "Your mother sent me to bring you home." But no matter what they say, never get into a car with anyone who is not a good friend.
   - If a stranger stops his car to talk to you or to ask directions, never get close enough for him to be able to grab you.
   - Never take shortcuts through lonely alleys, dark streets, or wooded areas. Also, don't play in empty, abandoned buildings or around new construction where there is no one to help you.
   - Never play near public rest rooms. If you have to use the toilet, go in quickly—with friends or an

adult—and then leave right away. Men looking for children often wait around such places.

- Unless you are with one of your parents, don't talk to strangers while playing in the park or shopping. Above all, never accept any treats from a stranger.
- If a teenager or adult sits down next to you in a theater, be alert. If he talks to you or tries to touch you, get up right away and tell the usher or the manager.

The above list of rules apply to girls and boys. Lists of prevention tactics for women are available from most local women's groups, and from the Washington, D.C. Rape Crisis Center (see page 137).

Long lists of rape-prevention tactics may make a woman feel that she must spend the rest of her life in total fear, but most are just a repetition of what most girls have already been taught directly or indirectly. Actually, one needs to be *cautious* more than fearful. Confidence in times of emergency has helped some women to protect themselves.

Again and again one must remember that each situation is different. As long as society is producing men who rape, women will find it to their advantage to follow some of the more common-sense suggestions. Since many rapes take place in the homes of women, adequate security seems to be a common-sense tactic. Using an initial on an apartment mailbox rather than a woman's first name is a tactic followed by many. Knowing people before allowing them to enter a house or

apartment makes sense. Requiring proper identification from home service men is important. Having keys
ready when returning home at night, and entering
quickly, is another good suggestion.

The best way to protect your body is by using your
head. Remember that the rapist frequently plans his
crime and watches his victim, waiting for the right
opportunity to strike. Don't give it to him.

Sometimes one cannot avoid being in lonely places.
In the following case, a mother of four in New York
City was putting out her garbage in an alley, when a
hand grabbed her at the waist. "Don't scream, I'm
armed!" the man shouted and began tugging at the
zipper at the back of her dress. This young woman was
shocked at the idea of what was about to happen to
her. As she turned toward the man, he seemed to melt
in with the alley and she became unconscious. A list of
rape-prevention tactics might not have helped her to
prevent this rape, for she could not avoid her chore,
nor could she control her loss of consciousness.

A rapist who only gets satisfaction from sexual
assault in which he feels power is sometimes deterred
by fainting, because an unconscious woman does not
provide such satisfaction. On the other hand, fainting
is not always the answer to protection or prevention,
for many rapists would prefer a woman who does
struggle.

It is easy to see that there is much disagreement
about how to protect oneself from rape. One man,
Frederick Storaska, author of *How to Say No to a*

Rapist—and Survive, suggests going along with the man until the opportunity to flee arises, but many authorities disagree with him. Some feel that playing along with the rapist to calm his anxiety may lead to physical harm, for when the woman finally rejects him, he may suddenly become *very* hostile.

Although relatively few victims of rape are murdered, no one knows how many are injured physically, and no one knows when a rapist will carry out a threat. It is typical for him to threaten to kill a victim if she does not cooperate, and to promise that he will not hurt her if she does. How often rapists attempt to carry out such threats, no one really knows.

Perhaps you are asking what a person can do when so much remains to be learned? Only recently has the general public become aware of the epidemic number of rapes which occur. Only recently has the education process begun to spread. How can one woman help to lessen the shock and psychological repercussions any woman who might be raped can suffer? How can one person help to change the attitudes of society in general? Lynn O'Brien McLaughlin of Jeffersonville, Vermont, is one example of a person who is making great strides in this area throughout her own state. She is bringing women together and instructing them how to organize rape crisis centers and hotlines. These will not only help individual women to cope with rape after they have experienced it, but may help to prevent rape through education and awareness. Lynn's original efforts came about as a result of participation in NOW,

where she chose the area of rape as a project. She
began meeting with groups of people in the city of
Burlington, Vermont, and then extended her activities
to other communities.

Many women want to do something but few know
how to go about it. Lynn obtained the cooperation of a
psychiatrist, an attorney, some social workers, and others trained in counseling. Out of this, a program of
training sessions evolved to encourage women in various areas of Vermont to develop their own programs.

The offshoots of the original group meetings are
developed into four types of workshops. The first
deals with the physical aspect of rape, another deals
with the legal aspect, the third deals with the psychological problems, and the fourth trains women in
counseling skills to help those who have been raped.
Each program differs somewhat according to the locality, but people travel long distances to the towns in
which meetings are held, and hotlines are spreading
throughout this mostly rural state. This is how it is in
many areas where the goals of NOW's Task Force on
Rape are being put into action.

In many communities, groups are gathering together under the direction of health departments, mental
health clinics, free clinics, women's groups, and other
organizations and are conducting workshops about the
psychiatric, medical, and legal implications of rape.
The purpose of such workshops is to educate and
sensitize community workers and people in general
about these problems. Agendas vary from group to

group but a typical one might cover the following areas:

1. The characteristic of the rapist.
2. The characteristic of the victim.
3. What happens in rape.
4. The emotional impact—short and long range.
5. Reporting the rape and how authorities respond.
6. Legal action that may be taken.
7. Response of the community.
8. Case material.
9. The role of community mental health services and other resources.

In such a workshop there may be a panel consisting of a medical doctor who specializes in obstetrics and gynecology, a representative from the state's attorney's office, a detective from the police department, a psychiatrist, and a representative from a local women's rape crisis center. The meetings are often informal, and sometimes videotaped programs are included to show interviews with a rape victim and give relevant information. Role-playing in which members "act out" rape situations helps participants to cope with actual problems.

Many colleges are taking action to help protect students against rape. There have been increasing numbers of assaults on students who study in the library late at night and walk home alone, or students who have evening classes and must cross unlighted paths on the campus. Bathrooms, dormitories, libraries, music practice rooms, and parking lots have all made settings for rapes. While many incidents go unannounced, Barnard College in New York City reported a student who was raped in her dormitory room. At City College in New York, there were reports of rape in a woman's locker room and in the shower. At George Washington University in Washington, D.C., an attempted rape was made in a bathroom, and the same man succeeded in raping another student who was walking from one dormitory to another at eleven o'clock at night (see page 95). The actual places where students have been attacked could make a long list. The NOW unit at the University of Florida at Gainesville has published a pamphlet which includes places to avoid on campus.

Other critical steps which have been taken at various colleges include the hiring of more security guards, the installation of better lighting on campus, the establishment of sign-in and sign-out rules in university-sponsored apartments, where dormitory visitors must leave some sort of identification at a security desk in the lobby. Some universities have tried a campus escort service in which male students volunteer to walk with women at night when they must go from building to building. Unfortunately, on some occasions the volunteers have raped the people they were escorting!

The campus of Wayne State University in Detroit has installed blue lights which mark hotline phones. As soon as the receiver is taken from the hook of a hotline phone, the university police can pinpoint the scene of trouble. The University of Chicago has installed a somewhat similar system with 100 white phone-boxes. At the University of Wisconsin in Madison, there is a woman-only taxi service called the Women's Transit Authority. Some college students feel it would be helpful if they could report rape to high level administrators even if the women decided to take no further action.

In investigations of sexual assaults on college women, it has been found that some of the rapists are fellow students who may even know the victim on a first-name basis. Other rapists are those who come to the campus specifically for the purpose of rape, knowing that students are friendly people and that it is easy to gain entrance to cafeterias or dormitories without being recognized as a non-student. One man who raped a female professor at the University of Chicago posed as a newspaper salesman and gained entrance to her apartment by forcing his way in at gunpoint. He then locked the door and not only raped the professor, but stayed for a short time afterward acting somewhat like a visitor. He even returned a week later as if he were visiting on a purely social basis, but at this time the professor had alerted the police and the man was arrested. He confessed to having come to the university community with rape in mind. Here again is an example of a rapist who seems to feel that the woman he victimizes enjoys both the rape and the company.

While many colleges are making efforts to protect students through the introduction of extra lighting, shuttle busses, escort services, emergency telephones to summon the police, and groups which help victims both through counseling and in their dealings with the law, only a few are trying to get at the roots of the problem. Many women feel that no matter how rape laws are changed or precautions are increased, rape will not be stopped. New attitudes on rape can only lessen the number and help the plight of the victim.

The Need
to Know More

If you are a woman, estimating your chances of being raped is a wild numbers game. According to some figures, your chances may be about 3.5 in 1000. Since most rapes still go unreported as mentioned earlier, and since the rate seems to be increasing, figures as high as one chance in ten over a period of thirty years have been projected for one large city. These estimates give very uncomfortable odds. No wonder many women are rising to the challenge and are trying to make rape an infrequent crime.

How can rape be discouraged? Dr. Shirley Feldman-Summers grouped suggestions for reducing rape in the United States into five categories. The categories overlap in some aspects, but they point up the various areas in which research can help provide guidelines for changes which may help to reduce the frequency of rape.

One approach is *changing society*. Feminists suggest that rape rates are high because men are taught to protect women and believe that they have "property rights" over them. Women are taught to be sexual objects, but, when raped, are accused of enticing men. By effecting massive changes in the societal attitudes, feminists hope to greatly reduce the number of rapes. Dr. Feldman-Summers does not know if such changes would stop rape, but believes that if some of the suggestions of the feminists would reduce it, research should be carried out in this area. "In terms of specific research questions, we need to gain a better understanding of the relationship between social norms, sex-role expectations, and sexual assault. This kind of research is difficult, but possible," she says. "If a clear relation can be found between rape rates and sex-role expectations, it would support the proposition that we need to provide different forms of sex-role education for our young people and re-educate others."

Another major suggestion for reducing the frequency of rape is a massive effort to change the behavior of the rapist and potential rapist. Dr. Feldman-Summers believes that we do not yet know what characteristics distinguish the sexual offender from the nonsexual offender except that the former assaults women sexually and the latter does not. A simple theory about the traits that characterize a sex offender is unlikely to be found. She suggests that the key factor in making distinctions will lie in the investigation of the "social environment" of the rapist and non-rapist.

Another major approach to the problem of reducing the frequency of rape lies in changing the behavior of the victim or potential victim. "According to this viewpoint," writes Dr. Feldman-Summers, "the behavior of the woman plays a substantial or primary role in whether or not she gets assaulted. As far as I know, no one has demonstrated that women who are raped are dressed any differently nor are they any more attractive than women who are not raped. Nor has anyone investigated what the impact of leading such a restricted life (not going to certain places at certain times dressed in certain ways) has on a woman. It is important to know what the effect of such advice is—are we punishing the potential victim for a crime she hasn't committed? In other words, are we hurting the victim more by restricting her freedom than is desirable?

"Although I am pessimistic about this approach (changing the behavior of the potential victim), there may be some truth in this point of view. If there is, we should learn it. This would require additional research focused upon the characteristics of the victim and her actions immediately prior to the assault."

A fourth approach toward reducing rape frequency is changing the environment. Campus precautions as described in the last chapter are examples of this. Better lighting, transportation, and increased police patrols may have some effect in the reduction of the number of rapes, but a great many rapes occur in homes where force or deception is used to obtain entrance.

Finally, Dr. Feldman-Summers suggests we change laws and judicial procedure. Since only a small proportion of the rapists seem to be apprehended and an even smaller proportion convicted under the old laws and procedures, there is little chance of rehabilitation. Nor do these laws deter potential rapists. But since legislation is reforming rape laws in many parts of the country, more rapists may be brought to court and the rape victim may seem less like the offender. But much research needs to be done before one can hope that apprehension and conviction of offenders will lower the frequency of rape.

Many women believe that lighter penalties for rape would help women to obtain convictions, since people on juries occasionally feel that the present penalties are too severe for the crime. Many feminists join those who feel that prison is not concerned with change but with punishment, and that the few men who are prosecuted act as scapegoats for the ills of society. Seeking alternatives is one of the goals of the Feminist Alliance Against Rape whose headquarters are in Washington, D.C. These women suggest helping those men convicted of rape to begin serious examination of their sex-roles. Educating men is viewed as a task of men, but women can act as catalysts in helping them to view rape as a violent, aggressive act against women. Some of the women who belong to the Feminist Alliance

Against Rape have already begun to meet with men in prison and have encouraged formation of groups such as Prisoners Against Rape. They hope that men will speak out in their communities to educate other men and conduct consciousness-raising groups. These men will hopefully join those who view the cause of rape as sexism, and will help to change the attitudes of society which they believe promote rape.

Certainly, there is a long road of research ahead before the rape problem can be diminished, let alone solved. But for all who give the subject of rape more than a passing thought, there are many things that can be done. Writing to representatives at local, state, and federal levels is the least of these, but it is an important step. It may help to promote the passage of bills that provide funds for research about rape, for better treatment of victims, and for better education. Even if you do not wish to become involved in a crisis center or a hotline, you *can* help by writing letters to create awareness of the problems that exist, and by helping to change attitudes among people you know.

For those who have in some way been affected more closely by this violent crime, the need for action now is well known. Hopefully, this book will encourage understanding, both of the need for research, and for action.

Suggestions for Further Reading

BOOKS

Amir, Menachim, PATTERNS IN FORCIBLE RAPE, Chicago, Illinois: University Press, 1971.

Boston Women's Health Book Collective, OUR BODIES, OURSELVES—A BOOK BY AND FOR WOMEN, New York: Simon & Schuster, 1973.

Burgess, Ann W. and Lynda L. Holmstrom, RAPE: VICTIMS OF CRISIS, Bowie, Maryland: Robert J. Brady Company, 1974.

Csida, June Bundy and Joseph Csida, RAPE: HOW TO AVOID IT AND WHAT TO DO ABOUT IT IF YOU CAN'T, Chatsworth, California: Books for Better Living, 1974.

Horos, Carol V., RAPE, New Canaan, Connecticut: Tobey Publishing Co., 1974.

Hyde, Margaret O., HOTLINE!, New York: McGraw-Hill Book Company, Second Edition, 1976.

MacDonald, John, RAPE: OFFENDERS AND THEIR VICTIMS, Springfield, Illinois: Charles C. Thomas, 1971.

Medea, Andra and Kathleen Thompson, AGAINST RAPE, New York: Farrar, Straus and Giroux, 1974.

Rush, Anne K., GETTING CLEAR, New York: Random House, 1973.

REPORTS AND PAMPHLETS

Freedom from Rape. Women's Crisis Center of Ann Arbor, Michigan.

How to Start a Rape Crisis Center. D.C. Rape Crisis Center, Box 21005, Washington, D.C. 20009.

Rape, Medical and Legal Information. Rape Crisis Center, Boston, Massachusetts.

Report of the Public Safety Committee Task Force on Rape. District of Columbia City Council, July 1973.

Report of the Task Force to Study the Treatment of the Victims of Sexual Assault. Prince George's County, Maryland, March 1973.

Stop Rape. Detroit: Women Against Rape, 1971. (18121 Patton, Detroit, Michigan, 48219.)

The Rape Victim's Dilemma: How to React. A Report on Rape in the Northern Virginia Suburbs. National Organization for Women, 1973.

GENERAL ARTICLES

Anonymous. "I Never Set Out to Rape Anybody." *Ms.,* December 1972, pp. 22–23.

Blanchard, W. H. "The Group Process in Gang Rape." *Journal of Social Psychology* Vol. 49: 259-266 (1959).

Burgess, Ann W. and Lynda L. Holmstrom, "The Rape Victim in the Emergency Ward." *American Journal of Nursing* 73:1741–174 (1973).

Calvert, Catherine. "Is Rape What Women Really Want?" *Mademoiselle,* March 1974, pp. 134–135.

Chappell et. al. "Forcible Rape: A Comparative Study of Offenses Known to the Police in Boston and Los Angeles." In *Studies in the Sociology of Sex,* ed. J. Benslin, pp. 169–190. New York: Appleton-Century-Crofts, 1971.

Chappell, Duncan and Susan Singer. "Rape in New York: A Study of Material in the Police Files and Its Meaning." 1973. (School of Criminal Justice, SUNY, Albany, New York.)

Evrard, John R. "Rape: The Medical, Social, and Legal Implications." *American J. Obstet. and Gyne,* 111:197–199 (1971).

Giacinti, T. and C. Tjaden, "The Crime of Rape in Denver." Mimeographed report. Denver, Colorado: Denver Anti-Crime Council, 1973.

Greer, Germaine. "Seduction is a Four Letter Word." *Playboy*, January 1973, pp. 80–82.

Griffin, S. "Rape: The All-American Crime." *Ramparts*, September 1971, pp. 26–35.

Goldman, J. "Women of Bangladesh." *Ms.*, August 1972, pp. 84–88.

Goldner, Norman S. "Rape as a Heinous but Understudied Offense." *Journal of Criminal Law* 63: 402– (1972).

Lanza, Charlene. "Nursing Support for the Victim of Sexual Assault." Washington, D.C. Nurses Association, *Quarterly Review* 39, No. 2 (1971), pp. 9–10.

Lear, Martha W. "What Can You Say About Laws That Tell A Man: If You Rob A Woman You Might As Well Rape Her Too—The Rape Is Free." *Redbook*, September 1972, pp. 83.

———. "Q. If You Rape a Woman and Steal Her TV, What Can They Get You For in New York? A. Stealing Her TV." *New York Times Magazine*, January 30, 1972, pp. 11, 55–62.

LeGrand, Camille E. "Rape and Rape Laws: Sexism in Society and Law." *California Law Review* #61: 919+ (1973).

Lee, Al. "Ways to Protect Your Home." *Better Homes and Gardens,* June 1972, pp. 16–28–29.

Lerner, Gerda, editor and author. "Black Woman Are Sex Objects for White Men." *Black Women in White America: A Documentary History.* New York: Random House 1972, pp. 150–161.

Lipton, G. L. and E. I. Roth. "Rape; A Complex Management Problem in the Pediatric Emergency Room." *Journal of Pediatrics* #75: 859–866 (1969).

Mickow, Glenn and Maureen Benson. "Group Therapy for Sex Offenders." *Social Work* 18, no. 4 (July 1973), pp. 98–100.

Schiff, Arthur Frederick. "Rape is a Form of Brutality and an Invasion of Privacy that Few Victims Can Forget." *Medical Aspects of Human Sexuality.* May 1972, pp. 76, 81–84.

Schultz, L. "The Social Worker and Treatment of the Sex Victim." In *Human Sexuality and Social Work,* ed. H. Gochras and L. Schultz, New York: Association Press.

Sutherland, Sandra and Donald J. Scherl. "Crisis Intervention with Victims of Rape." *Social Work* 17, no. 1 (January 1972), pp. 34–42.

"Victim in a Forcible Rape Case: A Feminist View." *American Criminal Law Review* 11: 335+ (1973).

Weiss, Kurt and Sandra A. Borges, "Victimology and Rape: The Case of the Legitimate Victim." *Issues in Criminology* 8, no. 2 (Fall 1973), pp. 71–113.

Werner, Arnold. "Rape: Interruption of the Therapeutic Process by External Stress." *Psychotherapy: Theory, Research and Practice.* 9: 349–351 (1972).

Appendix

Act No. 266
Public Acts of 1974
Approved by Governor
Aug. 12, 1974

STATE OF MICHIGAN
77TH LEGISLATURE
REGULAR SESSION OF 1974

Introduced by Senators Byker, Faust, Zaagman, Hart, Lodge, Bowman, Toepp, Novak, Pursell, Plawecki, Mack, McCauley, Zollar, O'Brien, Cartwright, Rozycki, Davis, Bouwsma, Brown, DeGrow, Rockwell, Richardson, Ballenger, Faxon, Cooper, McCollough, DeMaso, Pittenger, Bishop and Fleming

ENROLLED SENATE BILL No. 1207

AN ACT to amend Act No. 328 of the Public Acts of 1931, entitled "An act to revise, consolidate, codify and add to the statutes relating to crimes; to define crimes and prescribe the penalties therefor; to provide for the competency of evidence at the trial of persons accused of crime; to provide immunity from prosecution for certain witnesses appearing at such trials; and to repeal certain acts and parts of acts inconsistent with or contravening any of the provisions of this act," as amended, being sections 750.1 to 750.568 of the Compiled Laws of 1970, by adding sections 520a, 520b, 520c, 520d, 520e, 520f, 520g, 520h, 520i, 520j, 520k and 520l; and to repeal certain acts and parts of acts.

The People of the State of Michigan enact:

Section 1. Act No. 328 of the Public Acts of 1931, as amended, being sections 750.1 to 750.568 of the Compiled Laws of 1970, is amended by adding sections 520a, 520b, 520c, 520d, 520e, 520f, 520g, 520h, 520i, 520j, 520k and 520l to read as follows:

Sec. 520a. As used in sections 520a to 520l:

(a) "Actor" means a person accused of criminal sexual conduct.

(b) "Intimate parts" includes the primary genital area, groin, inner thigh, buttock, or breast of a human being.

(c) "Mentally defective" means that a person suffers

from a mental disease or defect which renders that person temporarily or permanently incapable of appraising the nature of his or her conduct.

(d) "Mentally incapacitated" means that a person is rendered temporarily incapable of appraising or controlling his or her conduct due to the influence of a narcotic, anesthetic, or other substance administered to that person without his or her consent, or due to any other act committed upon that person without his or her consent.

(e) "Physically helpless" means that a person is unconscious, asleep, or for any other reason is physically unable to communicate unwillingness to an act.

(f) "Personal injury" means bodily injury, disfigurement, mental anguish, chronic pain, pregnancy, disease, or loss or impairment of a sexual or reproductive organ.

(g) "Sexual contact" includes the intentional touching of the victim's or actor's intimate parts or the intentional touching of the clothing covering the immediate area of the victim's or actor's intimate parts, if that intentional touching can reasonably be construed as being for the purpose of sexual arousal or gratification.

(h) "Sexual penetration" means sexual intercourse, cunnilingus, fellatio, anal intercourse, or any other intrusion, however slight, of any part of a person's body or of any object into the genital or anal openings of another person's body, but emission of semen is not required.

(i) "Victim" means the person alleging to have been subjected to criminal sexual conduct.

Sec. 520b. (1) A person is guilty of criminal sexual conduct in the first degree if he or she engages in sexual penetration with another person and if any of the following circumstances exists:

(a) That other person is under 13 years of age.

(b) The other person is at least 13 but less than 16 years of age and the actor is a member of the same household as the victim, the actor is related to the victim by blood or affinity to the fourth degree to the victim, or the actor is in a position of authority over the victim and used this authority to coerce the victim to submit.

(c) Sexual penetration occurs under circumstances involving the commission of any other felony.

(d) The actor is aided or abetted by one or more other persons and either of the following circumstances exists:

(i) The actor knows or has reason to know that the victim is mentally defective, mentally incapacitated or physically helpless.

(ii) The actor uses force or coercion to accomplish the sexual penetration. Force or coercion includes but is not limited to any of the circumstances listed in subdivision (f) (i) to (v).

(e) The actor is armed with a weapon or any article used or fashioned in a manner to lead the victim to reasonably believe it to be a weapon.

(f) The actor causes personal injury to the victim and force or coercion is used to accomplish sexual penetration. Force or coercion includes but is not limited to any of the following circumstances:

(i) When the actor overcomes the victim through the actual application of physical force or physical violence.

(ii) When the actor coerces the victim to submit by threatening to use force or violence on the victim, and the victim believes that the actor has the present ability to execute these threats.

(iii) When the actor coerces the victim to submit by threatening to retaliate in the future against the victim, or any other person, and the victim believes that the actor has the ability to execute this threat. As used in this subdivision, "to retaliate" includes threats of physical punishment, kidnapping, or extortion.

(iv) When the actor engages in the medical treatment or examination of the victim in a manner or for purposes which are medically recognized as unethical or unacceptable.

(v) When the actor, through concealment or by the element of surprise, is able to overcome the victim.

(g) The actor causes personal injury to the victim, and the actor knows or has reason to know that the victim is mentally defective, mentally incapacitated, or physically helpless.

(2) Criminal sexual conduct in the first degree is a felony punishable by imprisonment in the state prison for life or for any term of years.

Sec. 520c. (1) A person is guilty of criminal sexual conduct in the second degree if the person engages in sexual contact with another person and if any of the following circumstances exists:

(a) That other person is under 13 years of age.

(b) That other person is at least 13 but less than 16 years of age and the actor is a member of the same household as the victim, or is related by blood or affinity to the fourth degree to the victim, or is in a position of authority over the victim and the actor used this authority to coerce the victim to submit.

(c) Sexual contact occurs under circumstances involving the commission of any other felony.

(d) The actor is aided or abetted by one or more other persons and either of the following circumstances exists:

(i) The actor knows or has reason to know that the victim is mentally defective, mentally incapacitated or physically helpless.

(ii) The actor uses force or coercion to accomplish the sexual contact. Force or coercion includes but is not limited to any of the circumstances listed in sections 520b (1) (f) (i) to (v).

(e) The actor is armed with a weapon, or any article used or fashioned in a manner to lead a person to reasonably believe it to be a weapon.

(f) The actor causes personal injury to the victim and force or coercion is used to accomplish the sexual contact. Force or coercion includes but is not limited to any of the circumstances listed in section 520b (1) (f) (i) to (v).

(g) The actor causes personal injury to the victim and the actor knows or has reason to know that the victim is mentally defective, mentally incapacitated, or physically helpless.

(2) Criminal sexual conduct in the second degree is a felony punishable by imprisonment for not more than 15 years.

Sec. 520d. (1) A person is guilty of criminal sexual conduct in the third degree if the person engages in sexual penetration with another person and if any of the following circumstances exists:

(a) That other person is at least 13 years of age and under 16 years of age.

(b) Force or coercion is used to accomplish the sexual penetration. Force or coercion includes but is not limited to any of the circumstances listed in section 520b (1) (f) (i) to (v).

(c) The actor knows or has reason to know that the victim is mentally defective, mentally incapacitated, or physically helpless.

(2) Criminal sexual conduct in the third degree is a felony punishable by imprisonment for not more than 15 years.

Sec. 520e. (1) a person is guilty of criminal sexual conduct in the fourth degree if he or she engages in sexual contact with another person and if either of the following circumstances exists:

(a) Force or coercion is used to accomplish the sexual contact. Force or coercion includes but is not limited to any of the circumstance listed in section 520b (1) (f) (i) to (iv).

(b) The actor knows or has reason to know that the victim is mentally defective, mentally incapacitated, or physically helpless.

(2) Criminal sexual conduct in the fourth degree is a misdemeanor punishable by imprisonment for not more than 2 years, or by a fine of not more than $500.00, or both.

Sec. 520f. (1) If a person is convicted of a second or subsequent offense under section 520b, 520c, or 520d, the sentence imposed under those sections for the second or subsequent offense shall provide for a mandatory minimum sentence of at least 5 years.

(2) For purposes of this section, an offense is considered a second or subsequent offense if, prior to conviction of the second or subsequent offense, the actor has at any time been convicted under section 520b, 520c, or 520d or under any similar statute of the United States or any state for a criminal sexual offense including rape, carnal knowledge, indecent liberties, gross indecency, or an attempt to commit such an offense.

Sec. 520g. (1) Assault with intent to commit criminal sexual conduct involving sexual penetration shall be a

felony punishable by imprisonment for not more than
10 years.

(2) Assault with intent to commit criminal sexual
conduct in the second degree is a felony punishable by
imprisonment for not more than 5 years.

Sec. 520h. The testimony of a victim need not be
corroborated in prosecutions under sections 520b to
520g.

Sec. 520i. A victim need not resist the actor in prosecution under sections 520b to 520g.

Sec. 520j. (1) Evidence of specific instances of the
victim's sexual conduct, opinion evidence of the victim's
sexual conduct, and reputation evidence of the victim's
sexual conduct shall not be admitted under sections
520b to 520g unless and only to the extent that the
judge finds that the following proposed evidence is
material to a fact at issue in the case and that its
inflammatory or prejudicial nature does not outweigh
its probative value:

(a) Evidence of the victim's past sexual conduct with
the actor.

(b) Evidence of specific instances of sexual activity
showing the source or origin of semen, pregnancy, or
disease.

(2) If the defendant proposes to offer evidence
described in subsection (1) (a) or (b), the defendant
within 10 days after the arraignment on the information shall file a written motion and offer of proof. The

court may order an in camera hearing to determine whether the proposed evidence is admissible under subsection (1). If new information is discovered during the course of the trial that may make the evidence described in subsection (1) (a) or (b) admissible, the judge may order an in camera hearing to determine whether the proposed evidence is admissible under subsection (1).

Sec. 520k. Upon the request of the counsel or the victim or actor in a prosecution under sections 520b to 520g the magistrate before whom any person is brought on a charge of having committed an offense under sections 520b to 520g shall order that the names of the victim and actor and details of the alleged offense be suppressed until such time as the actor is arraigned on the information, the charge is dismissed, or the case is otherwise concluded, whichever occurs first.

Sec. 520l. A person does not commit sexual assault under this act if the victim is his or her legal spouse, unless the couple are living apart and one of them has filed for separate maintenance or divorce.

Section 2. All proceedings pending and all rights and liabilities existing, acquired, or incurred at the time this amendatory act takes effect are saved and may be consummated according to the law in force when they are commenced. This amendatory act shall not be construed to affect any prosecution pending or begun before the effective date of this amendatory act.

Section 3. Sections 85, 333, 336, 339, 340, 341, 342 and 520 of Act No. 328 of the Public Acts of 1931, being sections 750.85, 750.333, 750.336, 750.339, 750.340, 750.341, 750.342 and 750.520 of the Compiled Laws of 1970, and section 82 of chapter 7 of Act No. 175 of the Public Acts of 1927, being section 767.82 of the Compiled Laws of 1970, and repealed.

Section 4. This amendatory act shall take effect November 1, 1974.

_____

Secretary of the Senate.

_____

Clerk of the House of Representatives.

Approved _____

_____

Governor.

THE BEST DEFENSE IS PREVENTION

SUGGESTIONS BY THE NEW YORK CITY POLICE
DEPARTMENT
SEX CRIMES ANALYSIS UNIT

PREVENTION IS THE KEY TO YOUR PERSONAL SAFETY
PREVENTION MEANS BEING AWARE—OF TWO THINGS:

1 What can happen to you
2 What can you do to avoid it

Greater safety lies not in getting out of trouble but in avoiding trouble in the first place. Self protection means taking all necessary precautions in order to reduce, minimize or possibly eliminate your chances of becoming a victim of a crime.

Women who live alone should list only their last names and initials in phone directories and on the mailbox.

The best lock cannot function if you fail to lock it. Be sure you lock your doors during the day, even if you are home, and even if you leave for a few minutes, (to walk the dog, get the mail, go to the incinerator, etc.).

Never open the door automatically after a knock. Require the caller to identify himself satisfactorily; this includes repair, delivery men, and Police Officers as well. Utilize chain bolt when checking identification.

Inside and outside lights give you a good deal of protection. Prowlers prefer the dark. Leave lights on at night, even when away from home. Change location of lights from time to time.

Leave light on door you will be using when you return home after dark. (Use timers). Have your key ready so that the door can be opened immediately.

When a stranger asks to use your phone, do not permit him to enter. Offer to summon emergency assistance or make the call for him.

If a window or door has been forced or broken while you were away, DO NOT ENTER OR CALL OUT, silently leave, use a neighbor's phone immediately to call police and wait outside until they arrive.

DRIVING

When practicable, travel on well-lighted more populated streets and thoroughfares. Keep windows and doors locked.

Do not leave your purse on the seat. Put it in a glove compartment or on the floor opposite yourself. Your purse can lure a criminal to your car.

Keep your car in gear while halted at traffic lights and Stop signs. If your safety is threatened, hold down on the horn and drive away as soon as possible.

Check your rear view mirror. If you believe you are being followed by another car, do not drive into your driveway, or park in a deserted area. Pull over to the curb at a spot where there are people, and let the car pass you. If the car continues to follow you, drive to the nearest place where you can get help, (gas stations, police station, fire house, etc.).

If you should be followed into your driveway at night, stay in your car with the doors locked until you can identify the occupants or know the driver's intent. Sound horn to get the attention of neighbors or scare the other driver off.

When parking at night select a place that will be lighted when you return. Check for loiterers before leaving the car.

Never leave car keys in the ignition even if you only parked for a short time. Take them with you, and make sure car is locked.

WALKING

After getting off a bus, or leaving a subway station, at night, look around you to see whether you are being followed. If someone suspicious is behind you, or ahead of you, cross the street—if necessary crisscross from one side to another, back and forth. If you feel you are being followed, don't be afraid to run. (One of the criminal's greatest assets is his ability to surprise you, to attack when you least expect it, by suddenly leaping out and not giving you a chance to fight back). Should he continue to trail you, be prepared to defend yourself by:

SCREAMING AND RUNNING—to a lighted residence or business, or possibly to flag down a passing car.

If a car approaches you and you are threatened, scream and run in a direction opposite that of the car. (The driver will have to turn around to pursue you).

Maintain a secure grip on your purse. Walk near the curb and avoid passing close to shrubbery, dark doorways and other places of concealment. Shun shortcuts, especially through backyards, school yards, parking lots and alleyways.

Have your key ready in hand, so your house door can be opened immediately.

When arriving home by taxi or private auto, request the driver to wait until you are inside.

Be sure you know the area you are walking in. Know what stores, restaurants, or gas stations are open late in the evening. If there are none of these watch for homes whose lights are on. If an attempt is made to attack you, run to these places and create as much commotion as you can. Create commotion by screaming as loud and as long as you can. It will call attention to your predicament and someone may call police or it may frighten the would-be attacker. (Yelling FIRE will also alert someone).

The way in which you carry your purse largely determines whether or not you are chosen to become a victim of a purse-snatcher. Do not carry your purse by the handle, or place your arm through the strap and let it hang. Place one end of the purse in the palm of the hand the other in the bend of the elbow. Draw it close to your body. Hang on to it firmly. The rule to remember is "carry as much money in your purse as you can afford to lose" when possible, hide the bulk of your money on your person.

PREVENTION MEANS BEING AWARE

ELEVATOR

If you live in an apartment where you know the other residents and you find yourself in the lobby with a stranger, you can let him take the elevator and wait for it to return for you. If you are on the elevator and someone gets on whose presence makes you uneasy, get off at the next floor. Always stand near the control panel; if attacked hit the alarm button and press as many of the other buttons as you can reach with your arm or elbow, enabling the door to open at any of several floors.

Never provoke an attack. If it is apparent that it is only your money at stake, give it up, try to remember what the perpetrator looked like, give as accurate a description as you can to the police. It is impossible to advise you specifically as to what to do if attacked, because only a person under attack is qualified to make this decision. The best way to avoid panic, is of course to be prepared.

Panic paralyzes you. If you are prepared to meet the emergency of possible attack, you are more likely to run (when that is the safest procedure) than if you are totally unprepared. Panic prevents us from seeing the possible solution to an emergency situation. Preventive procedures minimize the danger of physical attack. Take precautions; develop safety habits. Don't forget the best defense is *PREVENTION.*

Sources
of Further
Information

Feminist Alliance Against Rape, Box 21033, Washington, D.C. 20009 publishes a newsletter of national activities in protest against rape. $5.00 per year.

Contact local feminist groups for further information. Some of the groups listed on the acknowledgment page send information to those seriously interested in starting a rape crisis center, in developing defense techniques, etc.

Rape Crisis Center, Box 21005, Washington, D.C. 20009 publishes a number of helpful materials. Contact them for current prices of their bi-monthly newsletter, *How to Start a Rape Crisis Center,* Self-Protection Tactics, and other publications.

Women's Resource Center, 18700 Woodward Avenue, Detroit, Michigan 48203 may help you.

Women Organized Against Rape (WAR), Box 17374, Philadelphia, Pennsylvania 19105 offers some inexpensive publications.

Index